THE
A
RESTORATION OF ISRAEL

❦

A *STUDY OF HOSEA, AMOS, AND MICAH*

DAVID M. LEVY

THE RUIN AND RESTORATION OF ISRAEL

A STUDY OF HOSEA, AMOS, AND MICAH

DAVID M. LEVY

THE FRIENDS OF ISRAEL GOSPEL MINISTRY, INC.

THE RUIN AND RESTORATION OF ISRAEL
A STUDY OF HOSEA, AMOS, AND MICAH

BY DAVID M. LEVY

Copyright © 2008 by
The Friends of Israel Gospel Ministry, Inc.
Bellmawr, NJ 08099

First Printing 2008

ISBN-10: 0-915540-02-9
ISBN-13: 978-0-915540-02-0

Library of Congress Catalog Card Number: 2008922872

Cover design by Brenda Kern
Waveline Direct, Inc., Mechanicsburg, PA

Visit our Web site: www.foi.org

TABLE OF CONTENTS

HOSEA

AMOS

MICAH

PREFACE

Have you ever wondered why so many students of the Bible neglect the Minor Prophets? Perhaps it is their brevity. Or perhaps their content is viewed as antiquated, historical literature, penned millennia ago to a people buried in the dust of history. No doubt some view the messages as redundant, incomprehensible, and irrelevant to life in the 21st century. Unfortunately, the study of prophecy has fallen on hard times today and is not often preached from most pulpits. Yet people who neglect these books, for whatever reason, have deprived themselves of a rich blessing.

The Minor Prophets, especially Hosea, Amos, and Micah, are a treasure trove of practical truths, with timeless messages that speak to the human condition even today—morally, socially, politically, and religiously. These prophecies possess meaty teachings filled with godly principles and are by no means less significant than the rest of God's Word. These messages are as contemporary and convicting today as they were 2,800 years ago.

Judah and Israel, the nations to whom these prophets preached, enjoyed affluence and material prosperity. But political and moral corruption flooded the land. The court systems were corrupt, belief in God was superficial at best and tainted with heathen cults and idolatry, and the threat of war was imminent—much like our world today.

It is my prayer that the study of Hosea, Amos, and Micah will bless your heart, reveal insights that you have never seen in God's Word, and motivate you to share the truths found in these prophecies. It is my desire that getting to know these prophets will increase your love and support for Israel as it faces enemies in the Middle East focused on its annihilation—not unlike the days in which these works were penned. Lord willing, what you glean from these three prophetical books will embolden you to be a voice against the evils so prevalent in our world today.

David M. Levy

INTRODUCTION

God appeared to King Solomon in a dream and said, "Ask! What shall I give you?" (1 Ki. 3:5).

Solomon answered, "Give to Your servant an understanding heart to judge Your people" (v. 9). God not only granted Solomon's request, but also bestowed on him riches and honor so that he excelled all the kings of the earth in wisdom and wealth (v. 14; 4:29–34).

However, despite his wisdom and wealth, Solomon married many foreign women and allowed them to build altars in Jerusalem to their pagan deities: Ashtoreth, Milcom, Chemosh, and Molech. As time passed Solomon's wives turned his heart toward their gods. Thus King Solomon was not fully devoted to the Lord, as was David his father. The debacle that ensued was largely due to Solomon's pride, arrogance, idolatry, unbridled passion, and his neglect of God's law.

God revealed to Solomon that his disobedience would mean the destruction of his kingdom; after his death it would be torn away and given to a subordinate (11:1–13). The prophet Ahijah informed Jeroboam that God would divide Solomon's kingdom and install him as ruler over 10 of the 12 tribes (vv. 28–31). After Solomon's death in 922 B.C., decay, decline, and division came to the Davidic Kingdom.

King Solomon left the throne of Israel to his son Rehoboam, whose mother was an Ammonite. Rehoboam proved to be an arrogant, frivolous, stupid man who was totally nonreligious and untrained in God's law. The seeds of wickedness that Solomon had sown produced the fruit of rebellion against the reign of his son. The uprising began when Jeroboam, along with the congregation of Israel, requested that King Rehoboam ease the grievous burden of compulsory service and oppressive taxation that Solomon had levied on the nation. After counseling with the young men in Judah, Rehoboam replied, "My father made your yoke heavy, but I will add to your yoke; my father chastised you with whips, but I will chastise you with scourges" (12:14). In other words, the king intended to make Israel's burden even worse.

Upon receiving this news, the 10 northernmost tribes seceded from the Davidic Kingdom. Jeroboam, as prophesied by Ahijah, became the ruler of the northern kingdom (also referred to as Israel or Ephraim) with Samaria as the capital. And Rehoboam was left to rule over Judah (his own tribe) and Benjamin, the two southern tribes—including Levi—with Jerusalem as the capital. The northern kingdom expanded its borders, took control of the trade routes surrounding it, and became extremely prosperous. An upper-class society emerged in Israel and built expensive homes, enjoyed a carnal lifestyle, and exploited the poor. Corrupt leaders oppressed people and committed violence and robbery, while merchants chafed at closing their businesses for religious observances.

Jeroboam was not a religious man, but he knew Israel needed a god to worship. Yet he wanted to guarantee the people did not return to Rehoboam when they went to Jerusalem to worship the Lord. So he established an abominable nation of apostasy built on human wisdom, designed to eliminate any need for pilgrimages to Jerusalem to worship Jehovah, thus assuring undivided loyalty to his rule. He set up golden calves in Bethel and Dan and appointed degenerate men as priests (not of the Levitical priesthood) to sacrifice them in direct disobedience to God's law (12:27–33). Soon Baal worship replaced true worship of God in Israel. Jeroboam laid the foundation for the despicable behavior that would later evoke God's wrath and lead to Israel's eventual demise.

In this setting, God lovingly reached out to Israel by sending prophets to warn the nation of its apostasy. He sent Hosea, Amos, and Micah to confirm, condemn, and chasten Israel and Judah for their wicked ways. The Bible books for these prophets are not arranged in chronological order. Amos (760–755 B.C.) prophesied before Hosea (755–715 B.C.), who prophesied before Micah (736–700 B.C.). It well could be that Hosea, which emphasizes God's covenant love for Israel, was placed first in the canon of Scripture in hopes that Israel would see His mercy and grace before Amos thundered out his message of judgment.

Whatever the case, God pleaded with Israel to return to Him in repentance, forsake its sin, and live a life of fidelity within the covenant relationship He had established with the nation. But every attempt to woo the people back to uncompromising faithfulness failed. After warning the northern kingdom for more than 200 years, the die was cast for Israel's destruction. Guided by Tiglath-Pileser III (745–727 B.C.), Assyria began moving west to enlarge its kingdom, taking Israel in the process (2 Ki. 15:29). Israel revolted against Assyrian occupation and refused to pay tribute to the nation. Shalmaneser V (727–722 B.C.), Tiglath-Pileser's successor, invaded Israel and laid siege to Samaria. Although he died during the three-year siege, his successor, Sargon II (722–705 B.C.), continued it, capturing Samaria and all of the northern kingdom of Israel in 722 B.C.

Most of the Jewish people were deported as slaves to Assyria, which in turn repopulated Israel with Gentiles who married poor Jewish people who had been left in the land (17:1–41).

With the fall of Israel, only the southern kingdom of Judah and its capital, Jerusalem, were left. Judah, only a mere shadow of the once mighty empires of David and Solomon, consisted of the tribes of Judah, Benjamin, and Levi. Later the southern kingdom abandoned the Lord and exhibited the same spiritual, moral, and ethical decay of the northern kingdom of Israel. Sin had such a hold on Judah that it refused to heed God's message and ignored the warning it received through Israel's demise at the cruel hand of Assyria.

God was gracious to Judah and gave the nation more than 100 years to heed the warning, but to no avail. Jeremiah had predicted that Judah would fall to Babylon. In 586 B.C. Babylon destroyed Judah and Jerusalem and took the Jewish people into a captivity that was to last for 70 years (Jer. 25:11). Many prophets, especially such Minor Prophets as Hosea, Amos, and Micah, had warned both the northern and southern kingdoms. Hosea emphasized God's love. But Israel would not return to Him. Amos reminded Israel of God's demand for justice. Micah begged the Israelites to adhere to God's requirements for righteous living. His message was heightened by a promise that the Messiah would come and usher in the Kingdom blessings, long hoped for by the Jewish people, if they would only repent of sin and return to the God of their fathers.

The Divided Kingdom:
Israel and Judah

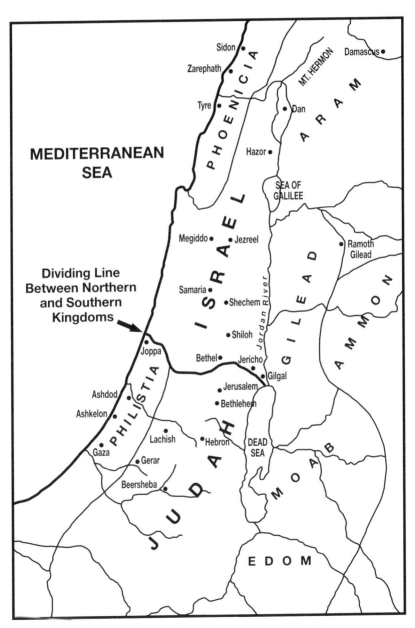

MEDITERRANEAN SEA

Dividing Line
Between Northern
and Southern
Kingdoms →

Sidon

Zarephath

Tyre

PHOENICIA

Damascus

MT. HERMON

Dan

ARAM

Hazor

SEA OF GALILEE

Megiddo

Jezreel

Ramoth Gilead

ISRAEL

Samaria

Shechem

Jordan River

GILEAD

AMMON

Shiloh

Joppa

PHILISTIA

Bethel

Jericho

Gilgal

Jerusalem

Ashdod

Bethlehem

Ashkelon

Lachish

Hebron

DEAD SEA

JUDAH

MOAB

Gaza

Gerar

Beersheba

EDOM

The Kings of the Divided Kingdom		
Judah (Southern Kingdom)		**Prophets**
Rehoboam:		
931–913 B.C. (17 yrs.)	1 Ki. 12:21–24	
Abijam (Abijah):		
913–911 B.C. (3 yrs.)	1 Ki. 15:1–8	
Asa:		
911–870 B.C. (41 yrs)	1 Ki. 15:9–24	
Jehoshaphat:		
873–848 B.C. (25 yrs.)	1 Ki. 22:41–50	
Jehoram (Joram):		
848–841 B.C. (8 yrs.)	2 Ki. 8:16–24	
Ahaziah:		
841 B.C. (1 yr.)	2 Ki. 8:25–29	
Athaliah (Queen):		
841–835 B.C. (6 yrs.)	2 Ki. 11:1–3	
Joash (Jehoash):		
835–796 B.C. (40 yrs)	2 Ki. 12:1, 21	**Joel** (830) Judah
Amaziah:		
796–767 B.C. (29 yrs.)	2 Ki. 14:1–20	
Azariah (Uzziah):		
792–740 B.C. (52 yrs.)	2 Ki. 15:1, 2	**Isaiah** (740) Judah
Jotham:		
750–731 B.C. (16 yrs.)	2 Ki. 15:32–38	**Micah** (735) Judah
Ahaz:		
735–715 B.C. (16 yrs.)	2 Ki. 16:1–20	
Hezekiah:		
715–686 B.C. (29 yrs.)	2 Ki. 18:1–20:21	
Manasseh:		
697–642 B.C. (55 yrs.)	2 Ki. 21:1–18	
Amon:		
642–640 B.C. (2 yrs.)	2 Ki. 21:19–26	
Josiah:		
640–609 B.C. (31 yrs.)	2 Ki. 22:1–23:30	
Jehoahaz (Shallum):		
609 B.C. (3 mos.)	2 Ki. 23:31–33	
Jehoiakim:		
609–597 B.C. (11 yrs.)	2 Ki. 23:34—24:6	
Jehoiachin (Jeconiah):		
597 B.C. (3 mos.)	2 Ki. 24:8–16	
Zedekiah (Mattaniah):		
597–586 B.C. (11 yrs.)	2 Ki. 24:17—25:7	**Babylonian Captivity** 586 B.C.

The Kings of the Divided Kingdom	
Israel (Northern Kingdom)	**Prophets**
Jeroboam I: 931–910 B.C. (22 yrs.) 1 Ki. 12:20—14:20	
Nadab: 910–909 B.C. (2 yrs.) 1 Ki. 15:25–27, 31	
Baasha: 909–886 B.C. (24 yrs.) 1 Ki. 15:28–34; 16:1–7	
Elah: 886–885 B.C. (2 yrs.) 1 Ki. 16:8–14	
Zimri: 885 B.C. (7 yrs.) 1 Ki. 16:15	
Omri: 885–874 B.C. (12 yrs.) 1 Ki. 16:23–28	
Ahab: 874–853 B.C. (22 yrs.) 1 Ki. 16:29—22:40	
Ahaziah: 853–852 B.C. (2 yrs.) 1 Ki. 22:51–53	
Jehoram (Joram): 852–841 B.C. (12 yrs.) 2 Ki. 3:1—9:26	
Jehu: 841–814 B.C. (28 yrs.) 2 Ki. 13:1–9	
Jehoahaz: 814–798 B.C. (17 yrs.) 2 Ki. 13:10–25	
Jeroboam II: 793–753 B.C. (41 yrs.) 2 Ki. 14:23–29	**Jonah** (780) Nineveh **Amos** (760) Israel **Hosea** (755) Israel
Zechariah: 753 B.C. (6 mos.) 2 Ki. 15:8–12	
Shallum: 752 B.C. (1 mo.) 2 Ki. 15:13–15	
Menahem: 752–742 B.C. (10 yrs.) 2 Ki. 15:16–22	
Pekahiah: 742–740 B.C. (2 yrs.) 2 Ki. 15:23–26	
Pekah: 752–732 B.C. (20 yrs.) 2 Ki. 15:27–31	
Hoshea: 732–722 B.C. (9 yrs.) 2 Ki. 17:1–6	**Assyrian Captivity** **722** B.C.

Note: Some kings in both Israel and Judah ruled under a coregency. Consequently, the dates do not always add up to the same number of years shown in parentheses.

INTRODUCTION TO HOSEA

Nothing is known about Hosea's background apart from his tragic marriage to Gomer and the children born through their relationship. The name Hosea comes from the word *Joshua* (Num. 13:16) and means "salvation." The prophet Hosea was not related to the last king of Israel who was named Hoshea (2 Ki. 17:1–6). The prophet's father was Beeri (Hos. 1:1), which means "expounder."

Hosea's literary style indicates he was an educated man, thoroughly versed in Israel's history and traditions. He wrote to the northern kingdom of Israel and was very familiar with its land, often mentioning Ephraim, Samaria, Bethel, and Gilgal (1:1, 4–6; 2:22; 4:1, 15; 5:1, 8). Hosea's prophecy was God's last warning to the northern kingdom before its demise; the nation's destruction came within a few years of this prophecy. Hosea also sent a warning to the southern kingdom of Judah (4:15, 5:5, 10, 12–14).

Hosea's ministry began around 755 B.C. in the reign of Jeroboam II (793–753 B.C.) in the north and culminated sometime during Hezekiah's reign in the south (1:1, 715–686 B.C.). The prophet ministered for at least 40 years (some scholars say 50), during the days of Jeroboam II, Zechariah, Shallum, Menahem, Pekahiah, Pekah, and Hoshea in the northern kingdom of Israel and during the reigns of Uzziah, Jothan, Ahaz, and Hezekiah in the southern kingdom of Judah.

At the beginning of the eighth century B.C., Assyria was on the decline and Jeroboam II was prospering; but soon the situation changed. During this time Israel became totally corrupt—morally, spiritually, politically, and socially (4:6–9; 5:1; 6:9; 7:3–5; 8:9–10). Assyria, guided by Tiglath-Pileser III (745–727 B.C.), began moving west to enlarge his kingdom, taking Israel in the process (2 Ki. 15:29). Israel revolted against Assyria's occupation but was soon defeated and most of the people deported to Assyria in 722 B.C. (17:1–6). Assyria then repopulated the land of Israel with foreigners from such areas as Babylon, Cuthah, Avva, Hamath, and Sepharvaim (v. 24). These Gentiles intermarried with a remnant of poor Jewish people who were not exiled to Assyria, and their children became known as Samaritans.

Hosea continued to minister after the Assyrian captivity in 722 B.C. God commanded him to marry Gomer, a woman who would become unfaithful and a "wife of harlotry" (1:2). Eventually she was put on the auction block to be sold into slavery by her lovers. Hosea bought Gomer out of the slave market, hoping to restore her as his faithful wife (3:1–3).

The prophet's marital relationship is used as a metaphor for God's relationship to Israel. In Hosea, Israel is pictured as the Lord's wife who committed spiritual adultery by leaving God the Father and chasing other lovers (2:2–5; 3:3; 4:10–19; 5:3–4; 6:10; 9:1). Israel pursued a lifestyle of spiritual adultery by practicing idolatry and worshiping the Canaanite god Baal. Hosea warned Israel again and again that unless it repented, God would destroy the nation. But Israel turned a deaf ear to his message (5:4).

Israel's defiance left the Lord with no alternative but to disown the nation as His people, resulting in Israel's destruction. In 586 B.C., the southern kingdom fell as well.

God will restore His relationship with the entire nation in the last days, after it returns to Him in repentance. Then and only then will He bring to fruition all the covenant promises He gave to the Jewish people.

The theme of Hosea is God's enduring love for Israel despite the nation's unfaithfulness. Such key words as *harlotry, idolatry,* and *unfaithful* express Israel's condition before God. Hosea 2:13–16 and 3:1 are key verses in the book. Hosea was a contemporary of Amos, Isaiah, and Micah.

꙳

OUTLINE OF HOSEA*

I. Gomer's Relationship of Infidelity (chaps. 1—3)
  A. Word to Hosea (1:1—2:1)
    1. Context (1:1)
    2. Command (1:2–3a)
    3. Children (1:3b–9)
    4. Compassion (1:10—2:1)
  B. Wife of Harlotry (2:2–23)
    1. Complaint (2:2–5)
    2. Chastening (2:6–13)
    3. Comfort (2:14–17)
    4. Covenant (2:18–23)
  C. Woman of Harlotry Healed (3:1–5)
    1. Command of God (3:1)
    2. Cost to Gomer (3:2–3)
    3. Condition of Godless (3:4)
    4. Call of God (3:5)

II. God's Rebuke of Israel (chaps. 4—8)
  A. Indictment of Israel—Revelation to Israel (4:1–19)
    1. Israel Indicted (4:1–5)
    2. Israel's Ignorance (4:6–11)
    3. Israel's Idolatry (4:12–19)
  B. Impending Judgment on Israel—Rejection of Israel (5:1–15)
    1. People Accused (5:1–4)
    2. Punishment Announced (5:5–12)
    3. Political Alliance (5:13–15)
  C. Invitation to Israel—Repentance Required for Israel (6:1–11)
    1. Israel's Immediate Response (6:1–3)
    2. Israel's Insincere Repentance (6:4–6)
    3. Israel's Immoral Rebellion (6:7–11)
  D. Iniquity of Israel—Review of Ephraim's Sins (7:1–16)
    1. Civil Rebellion (7:1–7)
    2. Chastisement Revealed (7:8–16)

E. Indifference of Israel—Reaping Judgment by Israel (8:1–14)
   1. Predicted Invasion (8:1–3)
   2. Pronouncement of Iniquity (8:4–11)
   3. People's Indifference (8:12–14)
III. God's Retribution on Israel (chaps. 9—10)
   A. Condition Described (9:1–9)
      1. Captivity Declared (9:1–6)
      2. Corruption Denounced (9:7–10)
      3. Children Denied (9:11–14)
      4. Coming Dispersion (9:15–17)
   B. Condition Denounced (10:1–14)
      1. Sin Addressed (10:1–11)
      2. Salvation Available (10:12–13)
      3. Sentence Announced (10:14–15)
IV. God's Relationship With Israel (chaps. 11—13)
   A. Israel's Disobedience (11:1–12)
      1. God's Call (11:1–2)
      2. God's Care (11:3–4)
      3. God's Chastening (11:5–7)
      4. God's Compassion (11:8–12)
   B. Israel's Discipline (12:1–13)
      1. Israel's Diplomacy (12:1–2)
      2. Israel's Discipline (12:3–6)
      3. Israel's Deception (12:7–13)
   C. Israel's Death (13:1–16)
      1. Detestable Religion (13:1–3)
      2. Divine Rejection (13:4–8)
      3. Destruction Reiterated (13:9–16)
V. God's Redemption of Israel (chap. 14)
   A. A Plea to Repent (14:1–3)
   B. A Promise to Restore (14:4–8)
   C. Appeal to Return (14:9)

*Outline does not always follow chapter titles or outline in each chapter.

CHAPTER 1

A NATION IN DECLINE

It was the best of times, it was the worst of times, it was the age of wisdom, it was the age of foolishness, it was the epoch of belief, it was the epoch of incredulity, it was the season of Light, it was the season of Darkness.

—Charles Dickens, *A Tale of Two Cities*

Dickens's immortal words depicted Paris during the French Revolution. They could also be used to depict Israel in the eighth century B.C.

History of Immorality

It was the best of times. Jeroboam II (793–753 B.C.) had enjoyed a period of military success, restoring "the territory of Israel from the entrance of Hamath to the Sea of the Arabah [Dead Sea]" (2 Ki. 14:25). Israel was experiencing peace, prosperity, and abundance. New temples and fortified cities were being built throughout the land (Hos. 8:14). On the other hand, it was the worst of times. With prosperity came a major decline in the religious, moral, and social order.

The Israel of David and Solomon's day had become a divided kingdom 150 years earlier when, led by Jeroboam, 10 tribes rebelled against Solomon's son, King Rehoboam of Judah. Declaring himself king over those tribes, which became known as the northern kingdom of Israel, Jeroboam I (931–910 B.C.) instituted sweeping changes in Israel's worship by building temples at Bethel and Dan and erecting images of a golden calves there that would later be worshiped. Thus he diverted people from returning to Jerusalem to worship.

Spiritual conditions worsened when, years later, King Ahab married Jezebel. With their marriage, Baal worship was introduced into the land. Such vile practices as religious prostitution, fertility rites, and the building of high places for image worship flooded Israel. Wrote Bible scholar Frederick A. Tatford: "Chambers and wooded areas were reserved for the sacred prostitution associated with the worship; male prostitutes (*kedishim*) being consecrated to Ashtoreth and sacred harlots (*kedeshoth*) to Baal" (Hos. 4:14; cf. 1 Ki. 14:23–24).[1] Thus people became victims of two false religions: calf worship introduced by Jeroboam I at Bethel and Dan, and Baal worship established by Ahab and Jezebel.

Israel's religious decline led to a rapid deterioration in its moral and social order. The leaders had accumulated wealth by corrupt business practices, perverted justice, bribery, robbery of the poor, and exploitation of widows and orphans. There was total compromise from the courtroom to the bedroom. Israel's deterioration was swift and extensive. H. Ronald Vandermey put it this way:

Justice was determined by the highest bribe (Hos. 7:1–2; 10:13), whereas faithfulness in word and deed was extinct (11:12). Drunkenness (4:11) and open harlotry (4:14) had taken on epidemic proportions. Established by God as a testimony of His standards (Exod. 19:4–6), Israel had become like her wicked neighbors, blatantly disobeying the laws of God (Hos. 4:2–3).[2]

With the death of Jeroboam II, political confusion and anarchy overtook the land. Jeroboam's son, Zechariah, was assassinated by Shallum after reigning for only six months. Shallum was assassinated by Menahem after reigning for only one month. Menahem managed to reign for 10 years. During that time, Assyria's Tiglath-Pileser III (745–727 B.C.) invaded Israel, extorted tribute from the nation, and made it a vassal state. Menahem's son Pekahiah reigned for two years and was then assassinated by Pekah. Pekah made an alliance with Syria against the southern kingdom of Judah. The Assyrians rallied in defense of Judah and captured Israel (732 B.C.). Hoshea assassinated King Pekah and became king over Israel. With the death of Tiglath-Pileser (727 B.C.), Hoshea stopped paying tribute to Assyria. An enraged

Assyria invaded Israel; and after a three-year siege by Sargon II, Israel fell in 722 B.C. (2 Ki. 17:5–6). Sargon deported 27,900 Israelites to the upper Tigris-Euphrates Valley and repopulated the area with Gentiles.

Hosea's Integrity

Out of Israel's depravity emerged the young prophet Hosea. He was a man of integrity and was well-educated, coming from the cultured class of Israelite society. All that is known about Hosea is recorded in the book bearing his name. His father's name was Beeri (v. 1); but no reliable information is given on his tribal identity, birthplace, early life, or occupation. His name means "salvation" or "deliverance" and is derived from the same Hebrew noun that forms the names Joshua, Isaiah, and Jesus. Ironically, Hosea was also the name of Israel's last king, Hoshea. Hosea was a contemporary of Amos, Isaiah, and Micah. Like these men, he was raised up by the Lord to rebuke Israel and call the nation to repentance and reconciliation with God.

Hosea prophesied "in the days of Uzziah, Jotham, Ahaz, and Hezekiah, kings of Judah, and in the days of Jeroboam the son of Joash, king of Israel" (1:1). He ministered through the reigns of the Judean kings mentioned and seven kings of Israel. Although scholars differ on the exact date Hosea began prophesying, he probably started around 755 B.C. and concluded sometime during the reign of Hezekiah (715–686 B.C.). It is not known why Hosea mentioned the four kings of Judah but omitted the six kings of Israel who followed Jeroboam II. Perhaps it suggests the legitimacy of the Davidic dynasty in contrast with the instability and illegitimacy of the kingship in Israel (cf. Hos. 3:5).[3]

The prophet's language is full of emotion and vivid expressions, rich with metaphors and similes and replete with illustrations reinforcing the impact of his words. His frequent use of plays on words, cryptic allusions, and subtle innuendoes provides fervor for his prophecy. Hosea's language soars into flights of poetry and descends into the pathos of grief, only to revert once more to forceful and logical arguments against Israel's sin.

Harlotry in Israel

Hosea received a strange command: "The LORD said to Hosea: 'Go, take yourself a wife of harlotry and children of harlotry, for the land has committed great harlotry by departing from the LORD'" (v. 2). The Lord's command must have startled and perplexed the prophet. Was God commanding him to commit adultery, something He had earlier condemned (Ex. 20:14)? It is doubtful that God would have done such a thing. Some scholars try to sidestep the moral problem of the infidelity of Hosea's wife, Gomer, by interpreting the verse as a vision, parable, or allegory used to illustrate Israel's relationship with God. Hosea, however, gave no indication that this account should be interpreted in such a way. The book of Hosea is a written narrative—not a vision, parable, or allegory—and should be interpreted literally.

Although the text is to be interpreted literally, that does not mean that Gomer was a harlot when she married Hosea.

1. Hosea wrote the text years after his marriage, which gave Gomer time to become unfaithful.

2. A righteous prophet like Hosea would never be instructed to marry a harlot.

3. If a woman was found to be a harlot before marriage, she was to be killed by stoning (Dt. 22:20–21).

4. Gomer was a virgin before marriage; but God, in His foreknowledge, knew that she would be unfaithful to her wedding vows.

5. The command, "Go, take yourself a wife" (v. 2) is a figure of speech known as a zeugma. This occurs when one verb is joined to two or more nouns but refers to only one of them. In this case, the zeugma involves the double verbs *Go, take yourself,* a Hebrew idiom for "get married." God was telling Hosea, "Go, take a wife who will prove to be unfaithful.[4] Hosea was to marry a woman with a propensity for sexual promiscuity. Thus the words are to be understood as stating her yet-to-be revealed promiscuity.

6. It is clear from Hosea 4:11–19 that God strongly condemns physical and spiritual harlotry.

7. In chapter 3, Hosea took Gomer back after she had been rejected for becoming a harlot. Hosea would not have been justified in rejecting her if she was already a harlot when he married her.

Hosea's tragic marriage to Gomer would serve as a living example of God's covenant relationship to Israel. God is explicitly portrayed throughout Scripture as a husband to the nation of Israel. Israel was unfaithful to God by giving its love to pagan gods. Hosea's own heartache as a betrayed husband provides an example of God's heartache over Israel's violation of its covenant relationship with Him.

God is portrayed in chapter 1 as withdrawing His love from Israel in the face of its pursuit of other lovers, such as the Canaanite deity Baal. Hosea's ministry was to describe God's indictment against Israel as spiritual adultery and to warn the nation that if it did not repent, it would reap the whirlwind of God's judgment.

CHAPTER 2

stop

THE MARRIAGE OF HOSEA

Hosea's marriage to Gomer and the birth of their children become the texts of God's message to Israel. Israel's unfaithfulness is portrayed in Gomer's infidelity, and the removal of God's covenant relationship with the nation is typified in the symbolic names given to Hosea's children.

God's opening command to Hosea, "take yourself a wife of harlotry," may lead one to conclude that Gomer was already a prostitute before she married (Hos. 1:2). However, that is unlikely. Gomer was probably chaste at the time of her marriage but possessed a propensity for promiscuity and was destined to become a prostitute over time. This command to Hosea can be interpreted to anticipate Gomer's future harlotry.

Hosea's heartache provides a visual analogy of God's own heartache over Israel. Like Gomer, who broke her marriage covenant with Hosea, Israel broke its covenant relationship with God by pursuing spiritual adultery.

Gomer bore three children who were labeled "children of harlotry" (v. 2). This reference does not imply they were the result of Gomer's extramarital affairs. It simply means that they would bear the stigma of Gomer's character and lifestyle. At the birth of each child, God instructed Hosea to provide names that symbolized the withdrawal of His love and mercy from Israel.

Prophecy of Retribution

Gomer bore a son to Hosea whom he named Jezreel (vv. 3–4). *Jezreel* means "God scattered" or "God sows." It is the name given to a fruitful valley that separates Galilee from Samaria, also called the Valley of Esdraelon.

Using the occasion of Jezreel's birth, God pronounced judgment on the house of King Jehu: "I will avenge the bloodshed of Jezreel on the house of Jehu, and bring an end to the kingdom of the house of Israel" (v. 4). Many years earlier, Elijah had prophesied that God would cut off the house of King Ahab and his queen, Jezebel, in the Valley of Jezreel because of their wickedness in killing Naboth and stealing his vineyard. Upon hearing Elijah's prophecy, Ahab humbled himself before God, and the Lord postponed the destruction of Ahab's dynasty until after the king's death (1 Ki. 21:17–29). Years later, under God's direction, Elisha anointed Jehu king over Israel and chose him to destroy the house of Ahab. It was in the Valley of Jezreel that Jehu carried out God's decree, slaying Joram and cutting off Ahab's dynasty (2 Ki. 9:1–37—10:1–17). For political reasons, Jehu went far beyond God's original decree and executed King Ahaziah of Judah, the princes of Judah, Ahab's officials, and the worshipers of Baal, a deed for which God would judge Jehu's house (9:24, 27–28; 10:11–14, 18–28; Hos. 1:4).

Jezreel's birth was not only a sign of judgment to the house of Jehu, but a sign of judgment on all of Israel. God announced that He would "break the bow of Israel in the Valley of Jezreel" (Hos. 1:5). This prophecy was fulfilled during the Assyrian conquest of Israel between 734 and 722 B.C.

Pity Removed

Gomer's second child was a girl. God instructed Hosea to name her Lo-Ruhamah. Some commentators believe Lo-Ruhamah was an illegitimate daughter of Gomer. This, too, is doubtful for it is the father's responsibility to name his child. The phrase *children of harlotry* was given to Hosea's son as well as his daughter, indicating that the daughter also belonged to the prophet.

Lo-Ruhamah means "not loved" or "no pity." God used the child's name to announce that He would "no longer have mercy on the house of Israel" (v. 6). He had suffered long with Israel's sin and had shown the nation His mercy and protective grace, but now that mercy would be utterly taken away.

Such was not the case with Judah, however: "Yet I will have mercy on the house of Judah, will save them by the LORD their God,... not... by bow,... sword ... battle,... horses or horsemen"

(v. 7). This prophecy was fulfilled when God miraculously delivered Jerusalem from Sennacherib the Assyrian in 701 B.C. Sennacherib surrounded Jerusalem and demanded the unconditional surrender of King Hezekiah. Hezekiah asked for time to consider the offer and took the matter to God in prayer. God answered the king's prayer when the Angel of the Lord delivered Judah by slaying 185,000 Assyrian soldiers in one night (Isa. 37:21–36).

Israel was to learn a number of lessons from this prophecy concerning God's protection of Judah. First, deliverance did not depend on national prosperity or military strength. Second, deliverance rested solely on "the LORD their God" (Hos. 1:7). Third, Judah would be shown mercy in time of looming disaster because it had put its hope and trust in God for deliverance.

People Rejected

Gomer's third child was a son whom Hosea named Lo-Ammi, meaning "not my people" (v. 9). The meaning of *Lo-Ammi* struck at the very heart of God's covenant union with Israel and revealed a total change in His relationship with the nation. The language of verse 9 negated a commitment the Lord had made to Israel during its captivity in Egypt: God (1) revoked His promise of Exodus 6:7, "I will take you as My people, and I will be your God," and (2) vowed to remove from the northern kingdom His providential care as expressed in the name by which He first revealed Himself to Moses, "I AM WHO I AM [Hebrew *ehyeh*]" (Ex. 3:14).

In Exodus, God emphasized His personal identity and announced to Moses that He had come to fulfill His covenant and keep His promise to deliver the afflicted posterity of Abraham, Isaac, and Jacob. In Hosea, God told the people directly, "I will not be the I AM [*ehyeh*] to you [Hebrew text]" (Hos. 1:9). Such strong words should have struck terror in the heart of every Israelite. God had severed the northern kingdom of Israel from any hope of deliverance.

Promise of Renewal

Had God severed His covenant relationship with Israel forever? No! Hosea assured Israel that one day God will reverse His declaration of abandonment and restore His covenant relationship with the nation. In the midst of Israel's rejection,

God gave the nation a word of hope framed in the promises of the Abrahamic Covenant.

First, God will *replenish* the world with Jewish people: "Yet the number of the children of Israel shall be as the sand of the sea, which cannot be measured nor numbered"—a fulfillment of the covenant God made with Abraham (v. 10; cf. Gen. 22:17; 32:12). This is quite remarkable, since the tribes of Israel are not identifiable today; but they will have an identity in the future (Ezek. 48:1–7).

Second, God will *restore* His covenant relationship with Israel and turn judgment into mercy: "It shall be said to them, 'You are sons of the living God'" (Hos. 1:10). Sonship restoration indicates that Israel will be spiritually regenerated (Ezek. 36:21–27).

Third, in that day He will *reunite* the 12 tribes: "Then the children of Judah and the children of Israel shall be gathered together" (Hos. 1:11). During the Kingdom Age Israel and Judah will be reunited into one nation (Ezek. 37:19, 22).

Fourth, the people of Israel will "appoint for themselves one head" who will *rule* over them nationally (Hos. 1:11). Scholars are divided on whether this ruler is King David or Jesus the Messiah (cf. Hos. 3:5; Ezek. 37:24). Scripture is clear: Jesus will receive David's throne and reign over the house of Jacob forever (Lk. 1:32–33).

Fifth, Israel will *return* to its land: "And they shall come up out of the land, for great will be the day of Jezreel!" (Hos. 1:11). This verse pictures Israel being replanted in its land (cf. Dt. 30:1–10). According to Hosea 2:23, the Lord has promised to sow the nation (Jezreel) in the land as one sows seed in the ground. The words *come up* (1:11) are translated "spring up" in other texts. As a plant bursts from the earth in all its glorious beauty, Israel sown in its own land will blossom gloriously in the Kingdom Age. Verse 11 closes with the words *for great will be the day of Jezreel*. It will be a great day for the nation when its judgment is ended and Israel is completely restored.

Hosea's message was to be circulated to other Israelites: "Say to your brethren, 'My people' [Ammi], and to your sisters, 'Mercy is shown' [Ruhamah]" (2:1). God will again embrace Israel, calling her Ammi ("My people") and Ruhamah (having obtained pity). These beautiful words express God's covenant relationship with Israel, and they will come to fruition at Christ's Second Coming.

CHAPTER 3

ISRAEL'S SPIRITUAL ADULTERY

Although chapter 2 tells of Gomer's unfaithfulness, the primary intent of the teaching is to describe in detail Israel's rejection of God and its unfaithfulness in its covenant relationship with Him. The text vividly compares God's relationship to Israel with Hosea's marriage to Gomer.

Chapter 2 encompasses the entire theme of the book of Hosea. Here and throughout, God deals with Israel in three phases. First, He charges Israel with spiritual infidelity for worshiping Baal and threatens judgment unless repentance is forthcoming. Second, He chides Israel's refusal to turn from idolatry, which later results in the prophesied destruction of the northern kingdom of Israel in 722 B.C. when Assyria carries the 10 tribes into captivity. And third, He reveals how, in the Great Tribulation, He will chasten Israel to full repentance and reconciliation and then restore the nation to peace and prosperity during the Millennial reign of the Messiah.

Charged With Infidelity

In 2:2 Hosea called on his children to "contend [KJV]" with their mother and bring a formal, legal charge against her for infidelity. The purpose was to motivate Gomer to end her adultery. Traditionally, a wife found guilty of infidelity was divorced or executed (Lev. 20:10; Dt. 22:22). But Hosea's goal was restoration, not divorce: "Go again," the Lord said, "love a woman who is loved by a lover and committing adultery, just like the love of the LORD for the children of Israel, who look to other gods and love raisin cakes of the pagans" (Hos. 3:1).

As Hosea had with Gomer, God had a legal right to disown or destroy Israel. But He, too, sought restoration by calling her to "put away her harlotries . . . and her adulteries" (2:2).

Chastening Implemented

After many warnings, however, Israel still refused to repent. God was left with no recourse but to chasten His nation. First, he would "strip her naked and expose her, as in the day she was born" (v. 3). Israel would be made needy and helpless, totally dependent on God as in the days of its wanderings in the wilderness of Sinai (cf. Ezek. 16).

Second, God would "make her [Israel] like a wilderness, and set her like a dry land, and slay her with thirst" (Hos. 2:3). He would withhold the precious water so necessary to produce food and sustain daily life.

Third, God said, "I will not have mercy on her children, for they are the children of harlotry" (v. 4). Again, this statement does not imply Gomer's children were illegitimate, but rather that they bore the stigma and shame of their mother's character and lifestyle. Similarly, all the children of Israel suffered when God removed His mercy and suspended His covenant relationship with them. Notice, harsh action was taken against both Gomer and Israel because both shamefully and passionately pursued other lovers: "I will go after my lovers, who give me my bread and my water, my wool and my linen, my oil and my drink" (v. 5). Israel even attributed its blessings to Baal instead of to God.

Fourth, God would isolate Israel: "I will hedge up your way with thorns, and wall her in, so that she cannot find her paths" (v. 6). Israel's exhaustive search for her Baals would end in futility and frustration. Today the majority of the nation still searches for peace and satisfaction apart from God. In weariness and despair, Israel will, in time, return to the Lord—her first "husband"— realizing that she had it better with Him (v. 7). Israel was blind to the source of its blessings: "For she did not know [refused to acknowledge] that I gave her grain, new wine, and oil, and multiplied her silver and gold—which they prepared for Baal" (v. 8). Israel not only attributed its prosperity to the pagan deity but also used God's good gifts in Baal worship. Therefore, the Lord promised to "take away" the blessings, producing shame and disgrace:

Therefore I will return and take away My grain in its time and My new wine in its season, and will take back My wool and My linen, given to cover her nakedness. Now I will uncover her lewdness in the sight of her lovers, and no one shall deliver her from My hand (vv. 9–10.)

Such "lewdness" (shame) was revolting to Israel's "lovers," none of whom were able to deliver the nation out of God's hand when He finally sent the 10 northern tribes into captivity in Assyria in 722 B.C. None possessed the ability or even the desire to rescue them. The same was true of Gomer.

Fifth, God judged Israel's feasts, which had grown so polluted and degraded by Baal worship that God no longer recognized them. His judgment resulted in the removal of all Israel's joyful religious celebrations, including "her feast days, her New Moons, her Sabbaths—all her appointed feasts" (v. 11).

Sixth, God vowed to "destroy her vines and her fig trees, of which she has said, 'These are my wages that my lovers have given me'" (v. 12). Vines and fig trees symbolize prosperity. Israel had regarded them as rewards in return for prostituting itself in Baal worship. So God promised to tear away the hedge He had built around Israel, resulting in the destruction of vine and fig tree (Isa. 5:4–7). As He said in Isaiah 5:6, "I will lay it waste; it shall not be pruned or dug, but there shall come up briers and thorns. I will also command the clouds that they rain no rain on it." Over time, the land would become an overgrown "forest" (thicket), given to "the beasts of the field" to eat (Hos. 2:12). In fulfillment of God's Word, the land did indeed lie dormant for centuries, devastated by soil erosion, swamps, and unproductive plants and trees and inhabited by wild animals.

Seventh, God judged Israel "'for the days of the Baals to which she burned incense. She decked herself with her earrings and jewelry, and went after her lovers; but Me she forgot,' says the LORD" (v. 13). Israel tried to attract and seduce her "lovers," a reference to sexual practices associated with Baal worship. In other words, Israel forgot the Lord. The word *forgot* does not refer to a mental lapse or loss of knowledge, but to a refusal to acknowledge the Lord's goodness, love, redemption, and authority. Israel totally ignored God's command not to run after Baal. Moses had continually warned Israel that judgment would ensue if it forgot God or pursued other deities (Dt. 8:11–20; cf. Lev. 26; Dt. 28).

Covenant With Israel

Despite Israel's sin, it is God who will ultimately take the initiative to renew His covenant relationship; and someday Israel will respond to the Lord's love and grace. Stripped of blessing, Israel will have nowhere to turn but to God Himself. Reconciliation will begin when God says, "Behold, I will allure her, will bring her into the wilderness, and speak comfort to her" (Hos. 2:14). He will take Israel away from her lovers and strip away the temptations of the world. In isolation, the nation will be able to hear God speak kindly to its heart with gentle words of encouragement that woo and persuade it to renewal and restoration. This prophecy will be fulfilled prior to the establishment of the Millennial Kingdom.

God also promises, "I will give her her vineyards from there, and the Valley of Achor as a door of hope; she shall sing there, as in the days of her youth, as in the day when she came up from the land of Egypt" (v. 15). Vineyards symbolize peace and prosperity. The Valley of Achor, which was a place of sin and defeat for Israel, will become "a door of hope" for all her Kingdom blessings (Isa. 65:10; cf. Josh. 7). In response, Israel "shall sing" the Song of Moses as it did when God brought the nation through the Red Sea (Ex. 15:1–21).

"And it shall be, in that day [Millennial Kingdom]," says the LORD, *"that you will call Me 'My Husband' [Ishi], and no longer call Me 'My Master' [Baali, or Lord]"* (Hos. 2:16).

In a renewed marriage to the Lord, Baal worship will be completely removed from Israel's mouth, mind, and memory (v. 17). Israel's renewed covenant and reconciliation to God will bring blessings to creation and the world (Rom. 8:20–22). Beasts, fowl, and creeping things that ravaged the land will no longer do so. God will reverse His judgment on the people: "Bow and sword of battle I will shatter from the earth, to make them lie down safely" (Hos. 2:18). They will not fear man or animals.

Freed from foreign invasion, they will live in safety and peace (cf. Isa. 11:6–8; 65:21–25).

Once again, the Lord speaks of a renewed marriage to Israel: "I will betroth you to Me forever" (Hos. 2:19). Betrothal in Israel was treated as a legal marriage (Dt. 20:7; 22:23–24). The permanence of this bond is assured by God's promise of "forever" and by each of these divine characteristics: His imputed "righteousness and justice," His covenant-keeping "loving-kindness" (Hebrew, *hesed*), His tender "mercy" (Hebrew, *ruhamah*), and His unquestionable "faithfulness" (vv. 19–20). Then, it is written, "you shall know the LORD" (v. 20). In that day Israel will finally understand and acknowledge her New Covenant relationship with God.

In the Millennial Kingdom, God will respond to the call of "Jezreel" (Israel) who calls to the "grain . . . wine . . . oil," who in turn call to the "earth," which calls to the "heavens," which call to the Lord to pour out needed rain for productive crops (vv. 21–22). God will reverse His judgment and restore all He has removed from the nation. A play on words is used: "Then I will sow her [Israel] for Myself in the earth [land of Israel], . . . then I will say to those who were not My people, 'You are My people!' And they shall say, 'You are my God!'" (v. 23). God will extend mercy to Israel and change the name "not My people" (*Lo-Ammi*) to "My people."

God will restore His covenant relationship with Israel, bring His people back into their land, bestow spiritual blessing upon them, show mercy to them, and once again make them His own. In response, Israel will cry out, "You are my God."

CHAPTER 4

REDEMPTIVE LOVE

How many people would be willing to buy back their own possessions? In all probability, not many. The average person today, it seems, would be more likely to spend twice as much money going to court just to prove that he shouldn't have to buy back something that was his to begin with. Then again, the average person knows very little about the sacrificial nature of true, redeeming love.

Following the birth of her second son, Gomer walked out on her three small children and her husband, Hosea, to become a prostitute. The main theme of chapter 3, however, is not about Gomer, but Israel. Hosea brings into focus Israel's past rebellion against God, its current state of isolation, and God's plan to redeem the nation in the future. In a simple yet touching way, God uses the story of Gomer, the wayward wife of a faithful prophet, to reveal the depth of His love for wayward Israel and for all who have sinned and fallen short of the glory of God.

God's Command

"'Go again,'" God told the prophet Hosea, "'Love a woman who is loved by a lover and is committing adultery, just like the love of the LORD for the children of Israel, who look to other gods and love the raisin cakes of the pagans.' So I bought her for myself for fifteen shekels of silver, and one and one-half homers of barley" (Hos. 3:1–2).

Some teach that God commanded Hosea to marry another woman. This position, however, cannot be supported from Scripture. It is clear from the text that chapter 3 provides a natural progression in the story of Hosea's marriage to Gomer. The word *again* can also be translated "yet," indicating that Gomer is to be the object of Hosea's love. The woman referred to in the text is the "adulteress," Gomer. If this were a reference to someone other than Gomer, the typological application to Israel as the wife of Jehovah would be lost or confused at best. Hosea's love for Gomer was to be modeled after God's love for Israel. Gomer, like Israel, was living in blatant sin when Hosea went to find her. And, like Israel, she expressed no contrition concerning her adultery and no desire to be restored to her husband. Instead of responding to God's love, Israel worshiped the Canaanite god Baal with "raisin cakes of the pagans." These raisin cakes were made from pressed grapes; and like the Canaanites, Israel used the cakes in its sacrificial feasts to worship and honor the "queen of heaven" (Jer. 7:18; 44:19). Such pagan customs polluted Israel's worship and greatly grieved God.

Gomer's Cost

Hosea did not think twice when God commanded him to purchase Gomer. He was willing to pay the 15 pieces of silver and the homer-and-a-half of barley to be able to bring her home. Fifteen pieces of silver was half the price of a common slave (Ex. 21:32). Some believe that the barley (a month's supply of food for a poor slave), along with the 15 pieces of silver, made up the price of a female slave. Many in Israel probably considered Hosea a fool for paying so much for a worthless woman. An unfaithful wife was divorced or executed (Lev. 20:10; Dt. 22:22); but Hosea's goal was restoration. In like manner, God has had a legal right to disown or destroy Israel; but He, too, seeks redemption and restoration.

God is called the Redeemer (Hebrew, *go'el*) of Israel throughout the Old Testament (Isa. 41:14; 43:1; 44:6; 47:4). The word *redemption* means "to deliver or rescue something by paying a price." It was used in reference to redeeming (1) Israel from Egypt (Ex. 6:6), (2) a person from slavery (Lev. 25:47–49), (3) the first-born males of man and beast (Ex. 13:11–16), and (4) an estate that had been lost. All these physical acts of redemption are not devoid of spiritual significance. They foreshadow God's redemptive plan through the Messiah.

The Old Testament concept of paying a redemption price is carried into the New Testament. Israel's long-awaited redemption, both physically and spiritually, is found in the person of Jesus the Messiah. Jesus made Israel's spiritual redemption possible through His death and resurrection (Rom. 4:25; 2 Cor. 5:18–19). His death paid the price to liberate Israel—and all mankind—from the slavery of sin.

The New Testament uses three Greek words to describe the work of redemption. First is *agorazo,* which means a price has been paid to buy a person in the slave market of sin's bondage (1 Cor. 6:20). Second is *exagorazo,* which means that the believer has been bought out of the slave market, or removed from the curse and bondage of sin (Gal. 3:13; 4:5). Third is *lutroo,* which means to "loose," or "set one free" from the slavery of sin (1 Pet. 1:18).

The story of Hosea's purchase of Gomer from a life of sin is a beautiful illustration of what Jesus the Messiah has accomplished for humanity, both Jews and Gentiles. God "has delivered us from the power of darkness and conveyed us into the kingdom of the Son of His love, in whom we have redemption through His blood, the forgiveness of sins" (Col. 1:13–14).

After Hosea purchased Gomer, he told her, "You shall stay [abide] with me many days; you shall not play the harlot, nor shall you have a man—so, too, will I be toward you" (Hos. 3:3). Although Gomer had been redeemed, she indicated no change of heart. She still desired her lovers and had to be taken into seclusion for a long time to prevent her from returning to them. The word *abide* means to "stay" or "sit in waiting" for many days. Thus Gomer was to remain isolated to force her to change her sinful ways.

Although Hosea reclaimed Gomer at God's command, he did not immediately become intimate with her again. It would take time to restore Gomer. The statement "so, too, will I be toward you," indicated Hosea's total commitment to his wife during her isolation. At the proper time, he would woo Gomer back to the love they once had for each other. Although God does not reveal Gomer's response to Hosea, most scholars believe her love for him was restored.

Gomer's isolation foreshadows Israel's isolation to deliver it from idolatry. Hosea 3:4 says, "For the children of Israel shall abide many days without king or prince, without sacrifice or sacred pillar, without ephod or teraphim." What does this verse mean? First, civil leaders, such as the king (ruling monarch) and prince (officers in the kingdom), were to be removed. Israel's sovereign political system would be destroyed and remain so for centuries. (Hosea was speaking about the northern kingdom).

Second, ceremonial religion was to cease. Israel's sacrificial system was to be eliminated because it was illegitimate and embellished with Baal worship. Setting up sacred pillars was forbidden by Jewish Law (Dt. 16:22). Third, cultic objects, such as the *ephod* and *teraphim*, were to be removed. The *ephod* was a beautifully embroidered garment worn by the high priest, over which was placed the jeweled breastplate containing the *Urim* and *Thummim* (Ex. 28:6–14, 30). After Israel's destruction the Israelites had no access to the high priest in Judah to discern God's will. The *ephod* referred to in this passage, however, is not the high priest's, but an image or idol used in fortune-telling. (See Judges 8:27; 17:5; 18:14, 17–20, 24.) The *teraphim* were small idols used in an individual's house for divination and necromancy.

The northern kingdom was stripped of all its civil leaders, ceremonial religious system, and cultic objects of worship. Like Gomer, Israel was to be isolated from its "adultery" and left in exile to meditate on its sinful ways. Meanwhile, said the Lord, "I will return again to My place till they acknowledge their offense"; and He waits for the nation to seek Him (Hos. 5:15; 6:1).

Commitment to God

When Israel's isolation is finished, the nation will return to the Lord: "Afterward the children of Israel shall return and seek the LORD their God and David their king. They shall fear the LORD and His goodness in the latter days" (3:5). God will use the terrible period yet to come, the Great Tribulation, to bring Israel to repentance and reconciliation. At that time a remnant within Israel will return to the Lord and receive Jesus as its Messiah (Zech. 12:10). The word *return* is used 21 times throughout Hosea's prophecy. Israel's return will result in God restoring "goodness," or covenant blessings, promised to the nation (Hos. 3:5). Then Israel will submit to the rule of "David their king."

The Davidic Covenant explicitly states that David's dynasty will be reestablished during the Millennium (2 Sam. 7:4–17). David's seed, the Lord Jesus Christ, will sit on the Davidic throne and reign over Israel in that day (Lk. 1:32–33). King David will return with the Lord to rule under Him during the Kingdom Age. The nation of Israel will "fear [tremble] the LORD," or hold Him in reverential awe, because of who He is and what they have suffered because of their rebellion (Hos. 3:5).

In the first three chapters of this book, the marriage of Hosea and Gomer served as an impressive illustration of God's grace and judgment. But as dramatically as Hosea and Gomer appear, they pass from this prophecy. In later chapters, Hosea said nothing about his personal relationship with Gomer but focused entirely on Israel's relationship with God.

God used Gomer's story to reveal His redemptive plan for Israel. Through his experience with Gomer, Hosea, no doubt, personally came to understand and appreciate the depth of God's feelings for Israel. Gomer served as an object lesson to Hosea, illustrating God's great love for His Chosen People despite their spiritual adultery and, indeed, God's great redeeming love for all mankind.

CHAPTER 5

INDICTMENT OF ISRAEL

Sowing and reaping is an immutable law of nature that holds true in both the spiritual and moral realms of life. The seeds of spiritual adultery and moral deviance sown in Israel during the reign of King Jeroboam II produced a crop of religious and social corruption that propelled the nation on a steady downward course. It became only a matter of time before Israel would reap God's judgment, resulting in its destruction. The nation's sins are depicted in graphic language in the remaining chapters of the book of Hosea.

Israel Indicted

Hosea delivered a subpoena from God that indicted Israel for its reprehensible wickedness. In a loud voice, Hosea cried, "Hear the word of the LORD, you children of Israel, for the LORD brings a charge against the inhabitants of the land: 'There is no truth or mercy or knowledge of God in the land'" (Hos. 4:1). The subpoena figuratively summoned Israel to appear in court to address the charge of breaking God's covenant and commandments. God was not only the Prosecuting Attorney but also the Judge who would pass sentence on Israel. The indictment charged the nation with a threefold failure to exhibit the spiritual qualities that should have characterized the people of God; and they broke five of the Ten Commandments.

First, Israel was charged with a lack of truth in speech and actions (v. 1). The word truth (Hebrew, *emeth*) means "faithfulness, reliability," and "stability." Without integrity in character and conduct, there would be no stability in the land. Second,

Israel was charged with a lack of mercy (v. 1). The Hebrew word for "mercy" (*hesed*) can also be translated "loving-kindness, goodness," or "pity." From the ruling king to the man on the street, no one evidenced either natural affection or compassion for one another. Third, Israel was charged with having no knowledge of God (v. 1). Israel had access to the knowledge of God through the Mosaic Law, but it did not practice the principles set forth in the Law nor pass them down to the next generation. Over time, moral and religious corruption replaced godly behavior, leaving the nation devoid of inward spiritual conviction and bereft of understanding concerning God's ways and purposes. Truth and mercy are two basic attributes of God's divine nature and must be reflected in the social ethics of any people, or they will not survive.

The natural consequence of Israel's blatant rebellion against God was that it broke five of the Ten Commandments: "swearing [calling down curses on people] and lying, killing and stealing and committing adultery" (v. 2). These are the third, ninth, sixth, eighth, and seventh commandments (Ex. 20:7, 16, 13, 15, and 14 respectively). Iniquity and murder swept the land as "bloodshed upon bloodshed" (Hos. 4:2). All these sins spontaneously flooded across Israel, contaminating everything in sight.

Israel's moral depravity even affected nature: "Therefore the land will mourn; and everyone who dwells there will waste away . . . beasts . . . birds . . . [and] fish . . . will be taken away" (v. 3). The land would cry out as crops withered and animal life perished for lack of water and food. Moses prophesied that these judgments would come if Israel turned away from God (Lev. 26; Dt. 28).

Inevitably, people began to blame one another for the deteriorating conditions. And they especially blamed the priests and prophets. However, God put a stop to that: "Now let no man contend [strive], or rebuke another; for your people are like those who contend [strive] with the priest" (Hos. 4:4). Though the priests and prophets were guilty of causing the people to stumble, God forbade the people to bring recrimination against them (cf. Dt. 17:8–12) because they, too, were as much to blame for conditions within the land. God held all responsible for the fall of Israel: priests, prophets, and populace alike.

With the court proceedings ended and the guilty verdict returned, sentence against Israel was ready to be carried out: "Therefore you [priests] shall stumble [fall] in the day; the prophet also shall stumble [fall] with you in the night; and I will destroy your mother" (v. 5). The phrase *your mother* refers to God cutting off the nation as a whole. This happened in 722 B.C. when the Assyrian army destroyed Israel (the 10 northern tribes) and carried its people into captivity.

Israel's Ignorance

The primary responsibility of the priests was to teach Israel the knowledge of God's Word and His Law so that the nation would know how to worship and serve the Lord. But the priests had willfully rejected God's knowledge and failed to teach it to the people.

"My people are destroyed for lack of knowledge. Because you have rejected knowledge, I also will reject you from being priest for Me; because you have forgotten the law of your God, I also will forget your children" (v. 6). Since the priests had rejected knowledge, God would reject the priests. And because they had forgotten the law of God, He would forget their children. Thus the sons of the priests would not inherit the office of their fathers, bringing to an end the priesthood in Israel. This did not mean, however, that the priesthood in Judah would cease; it would remain intact until A.D. 70.

As the priests of Israel increased, growing in number and wealth, the greater their sin grew: "The more they increased, the more they sinned against Me," said God (v. 7). Their sin increased in two ways. First, the Hebrew word for "sin" (*chattath*) can be translated "sin offering," meaning the more sin offerings they presented in idolatrous worship, the more their condemnation multiplied before God. Second, the priests "eat up the sin of My people; they set their heart on their iniquity" (v. 8). The priests turned the offerings that were intended for God into a thriving little business for themselves. They received a portion of every animal sacrificed, along with a fee for their services. Thus they literally and metaphorically fed off the sacrifice. The more the Israelites sinned, the more sacrifices they offered, and the more the priests profited. Though they were religious leaders, they made no attempt to teach people about the holiness of God or to deter them from a life of sin. Rather, they encouraged iniquity for their own personal gain. Therefore, God changed "their glory into shame [disgrace]" (v. 7).

Hosea continued: "And it shall be: like people, like priest. So I will punish them for their ways, and reward them their deeds" (v. 9). The priests and the people were addressed as one man. And both would receive the same punishment.

God's judgment against the priests would unfold in three ways: First, "They shall eat, but not have enough" (v. 10). The priests who greedily fed off the sin offerings would be left unsatisfied with what they received. Second, "They shall commit harlotry, but not increase" (v. 10). Those who practiced so-called sacred prostitution in connection with the worship of Baal, the Caananite fertility god, and encouraged Israel to obtain fertility of the soil and womb by doing likewise, would be "rewarded" with childlessness. Third, "Harlotry, wine, and new wine [would] enslave [their] heart" (v. 11). The word *heart* signifies affections, understanding, and rational thinking. Most priests were addicted to wine and sexual perversion, both of which affected their minds and bodies. They became mentally dull, spiritually ignorant and indifferent, and devoid of natural affection for one another. The priests sowed perversion, and the people of Israel reaped the dreadful results.

Israel's Idolatry

The priests and the general public were so possessed by a spirit of harlotry that they asked "counsel from their wooden idols, and their staff" (v. 12). Rather than seeking God, Israel sought direction through divination before inanimate wood idols with a diviner's staff. The "spirit of harlotry" caused the Israelites to offer "sacrifices on the mountaintops, and burn incense on the hills, under oaks, poplars, and terebinths [elms]" (v. 13). Even worse, the daughters and wives followed the example of their fathers and husbands by practicing "sacred" prostitution; "Your daughters commit harlotry, and your brides commit adultery" (v. 13). God would not single out the daughters and spouses for judgment, because the men of Israel committed the same sin: "For the men themselves go apart with harlots, and offer sacrifices with a ritual harlot" (v. 14). Tragically, these people who "do not understand will be trampled" (v. 14). Israel's perversion and lack of spiritual understanding led to its destruction.

After speaking about the northern tribes of Israel, Hosea abruptly turned to Judah and warned the southern kingdom not to follow in Israel's footsteps. He also warned Judah not to make oaths to the Lord in a place of idolatry: "Let not Judah offend. Do not come up to Gilgal, nor go up to Beth Aven, nor swear an oath, saying, 'As the LORD lives'" (v. 15). Gilgal was located in Samaria and was a holy place until Israel desecrated it with idols. The name Beth Aven ("house of wickedness," i.e., wickedness or idolatry) is a substitute for the name Bethel ("house of God")—another holy place, where the Lord had appeared to Jacob. God was condemning the practice of idolatry in these cities and warned Judah not to visit such places in Israel.

Israel also worshiped cows, which were a portrait of Israel—a young "stubborn [rebellious] calf" that refused to be led by the Lord (v. 16). God vowed to give His people their way and to "let them forage like a lamb in open country" (v. 16). Like a lamb in a large field, without protective boundaries or guiding shepherd, they would be consigned to wander the world, unprotected from predators who would try to destroy them. Hosea cried out to a rebellious Israel, "Ephraim is joined [yoked] to idols, let him alone" (v. 17). Ephraim was the largest and most prominent of the 10 tribes, and the name is used throughout the book of Hosea to refer to the northern kingdom. Since Israel was so inextricably yoked to idolatry, God instructed other nations to have nothing to do with it and not to intervene when Israel's judgment came.

Thus Israel's leaders brought the nation to shame by their excessive drinking and immorality: "Their drink is rebellion, they commit harlotry continually. Her rulers dearly love dishonor" (v. 18). The word *rulers* means "shields" and describes the leaders' protective role as guardians of Israel. But instead of guarding Israel from evil, they promoted the very wickedness that brought the nation to shame, not glory.

Hosea closed this indictment with a prediction of Israel's sudden destruction: "The wind has wrapped her up in its wings, and they shall be ashamed because of their sacrifices" (v. 19). As prophesied, the Assyrians came like a whirlwind in 722 B.C. and carried helpless Israel into captivity. In exile, Israel had years to reflect on its idolatrous sacrifices, sinful lifestyle, and shameful deeds.

Although all this transpired long ago, no nation is exempt from what happened to Israel. God is forever consistent in applying His eternal, immutable, divine law of sowing and reaping. No nation can escape. Whatsoever is sown shall, in due time, also be reaped.

CHAPTER 6

IMPENDING JUDGMENT

Batsell B. Baxter tells of a huge painting hanging in the Supreme Court Building of Switzerland. In the foreground are the litigants who have come to the court seeking justice. Above them are seated the Swiss judges, robed in black. By what criteria will they pronounce judgment? The artist's answer is simple: There stands Justice (usually depicted as blindfolded, her sword held vertically) with her eyes opened wide and her sword pointing downward to an open book on which is written "The Word of God."

The standard of judgment in this painting was also God's standard when He judged Israel in the days of the prophet Hosea. Israel was guilty of breaking the Mosaic Law found in God's Word. Hosea chapter 5 expands the basic themes of God's indictment against Israel.

People Accused

Though all of Israel was guilty, God blamed the nation's leadership for ensnaring the people in sin. Hosea cried out, "Hear this, O priests! Take heed, O house of Israel! Give ear, O house of the king! For yours is the judgment, because you have been a snare to Mizpah and a net spread on Tabor" (Hos. 5:1).

Judgment would befall the priests, the general public, and the political leaders alike. But God considered the priests and political leaders to be the greater transgressors. By failing to teach the people God's law, the priests were guilty of ensnaring the nation in sin. And the leadership, weakened by self indulgent sins, was unable to provide guidance and direction. Ironically, those who were to teach about judgment (priests) and to execute justice (princes) were now the subjects of judgment.

There were three charges leveled against the leaders of Israel. (1) THEY WERE A SNARE. Scripture says they were a "snare to Mizpah" (v. 1). (2) THEY WERE A NET. They were also a "net spread on Tabor" (v. 1). Israel had been snared, or trapped, like an animal and netted, or entangled, like a bird into heathen worship at cultic sites dedicated to Baal. The word *mizpah* means "watchtower." There were at least five places throughout the land called Mizpah. The two most famous were Mizpah in Gilead, east of the Jordan, where Jacob and Laban made a covenant before God (Gen. 31:45–55) and Mizpah west of the Jordan that was a border town in Benjamin between Judah and Israel. Mount Tabor is located in northern Israel, southwest of the Sea of Galilee. Mizpah in the south and Mount Tabor in the north were high places in the land and symbolized the heathen worship Israel practiced in every area of the country. Instead of safeguarding the people of Israel, the priests and princes had seduced them by entrapping and entangling them in sin throughout the land—north, south, east, and west.

(3) THEY WERE REVOLTERS. God said these "revolters are deeply involved in slaughter, though I rebuke them all" (Hos. 5:2). Those sacrificing to Baal had become so thoroughly involved in slaying and sacrificing to idols that they brought destructive consequences on the common people of the land. Idolatry warranted God's rebuke (chastening) of all Israel.

Some teach that the word *rebuke* refers to God pouring out His wrath in a punishment just short of Israel's annihilation as a people. Others believe it means severe punishment tempered by God's love and mercy with a view to correcting their idolatry. Whenever God chastened the Israelites, it was with two objectives in mind: to punish them for sin and to bring them to repentance.

Israel's sin was not hidden from God: "I know Ephraim, and Israel is not hidden from Me; for now, O Ephraim, you commit harlotry; Israel is defiled" (v. 3). No matter how hard a person or nation tries to conceal sin, God sees it and can reveal it. Moses told Israel, "Be sure your sin will find you out" (Num. 32:23).

Ephraim was the most powerful tribe in the northern kingdom. It was Ephraim that led and influenced the other nine tribes to participate so entirely in the sin that defiled them.

But nothing was hidden from the eyes of the Almighty, and Israel's sin was like an open sore in His sight. Israel's idolatrous worship centers adorned every high place in Israel, and the nation indulged in pagan worship that was accented by sexual immorality that God called harlotry. The nation had reached a point of no return; judgment was certain.

Hosea said, "They do not direct their deeds toward turning to their God, for the spirit of harlotry is in their midst, and they do not know the LORD" (Hos. 5:4). In other words, the Israelites' evil doings prevented them from turning to God in repentance. Therefore, they were locked into judgment, with no place to turn to escape the impending punishment. The "spirit of harlotry" had enslaved them, making them incapable of reversing their course of action.

Here was a nation privileged above all others in the knowledge of God. God had revealed Himself to Israel, made a covenant with it, and given Israel the Law. Yet despite all this blessing, Israel had ignored God and thus become ignorant of God's ways and His desire for repentance.

Punishment Announced

The result of sin would be that "the pride of Israel testifies to his face; therefore Israel and Ephraim stumble in their iniquity; Judah also stumbles with them" (v. 5). The phrase *pride of Israel* can be interpreted two ways. The first is that God, who is the pride of Israel, would withdraw Himself from the sinful nation that ignored Him and would testify, or bear witness, against it through judgment. The second is that Israel's pride, or self-reliance, would testify, or bear legal witness, against the nation. The latter interpretation better suits the context of the passage. It was pride and iniquity that brought both the northern and southern kingdoms to judgment.

One day Israel would wake up to its condition and seek the Lord: "With their flocks and herds they shall go to seek the LORD, but they will not find Him; He has withdrawn Himself from them" (v. 6). With numerous and costly sacrifices, Israel would seek forgiveness and favor from God, but its works would be in vain because its repentance would be insincere. So God withdrew His presence from the nation. How true the Scripture that says obedience is better than sacrifice (1 Sam. 15:22).

Hosea continued: "They have dealt treacherously with the LORD, for they have begotten pagan children. Now a New Moon shall devour them and their heritage" (Hos. 5:7). Israel's infidelity in practicing cultic worship produced "pagan children," or illegitimate offspring, who would reflect the wicked works and ways of their parents. The Israelites had practiced sexual fertility rights through Baal worship in the hope that they would have a productive harvest. In reality, their sinful practices resulted in their destruction and that of their crops.

Israel's destruction was fast approaching. The Assyrian army was already on the march. The watchman was to "blow the ram's horn in Gibeah, the trumpet in Ramah! Cry aloud at Beth Aven, 'Look behind you, O Benjamin!'" (v. 8). Gibeah and Ramah were strategic cities in Benjamin, and Beth Aven (Bethel) was the southernmost area in the northern kingdom, since it was on the border of Israel and Judah. The southern kingdom was to be on the alert that the invading army was almost at its doorstep and had arrived at the kingdom's border.

The outcome was certain: "Ephraim shall be desolate in the day of rebuke; among the tribes of Israel I make known what is sure," said the Lord (v. 9). God affirmed through Hosea that Israel would be made desolate in the day of judgment, a literal fulfillment of Leviticus 26:32–35.

Judah was not to rejoice over Israel's destruction for in time, it, too, would be destroyed. Judah was guilty of moving landmark stones that divided property between neighbors, and it would be judged for its actions: "The princes of Judah are like those who remove a landmark; I will pour out my wrath on them like water," the Lord said (Hos. 5:10). The Mosaic Law forbade anyone, even kings and high officials, to move boundaries and pronounced a curse on those who did so (Dt. 19:14; 27:17).

Some believe the crime of moving landmarks is metaphoric and is meant to cover all social injustices practiced by Judah's leaders.

In Hosea 5:11, the Lord abruptly returns to the theme of judgment on Ephraim: "Ephraim is oppressed and broken [crushed] in judgment, because he willingly walked by human precept [after the commandment]." This is the tragedy Moses prophesied would come on Israel if it rejected God's commandments and statutes (Dt. 28:33). The phrase *walked by human precept* could refer to following King Jeroboam's command to worship the two golden calves he had placed in Bethel and Dan (1 Ki. 12:28–29). It was this sin that precipitated Israel's downfall.

Speaking to both Israel and Judah, God said, "Therefore I will be to Ephraim like a moth, and to the house of Judah like rottenness" (Hos. 5:12). As a moth slowly and silently eats away a woolen garment, so would God consume Ephraim. Judah, like a piece of wood, would silently decay from "rottenness" on the inside. The demise of Israel and Judah had begun long before this point in their history; and both would be consumed and carried into captivity—but Judah more slowly.

Political Alliance

Israel and Judah were acutely aware of their disease and likely demise. Yet Ephraim did not seek the Lord, but went "to Assyria and sent to King Jareb" for help and healing (v. 13). The phrase *King Jareb* means "warrior king" and might refer to the time Israel's King Menahem or King Hoshea made an alliance with Assyria (2 Ki. 15:19–20; 17:3). "Judah saw his wound" and, during the reign of Ahaz, sought help from Tiglath-Pileser III (Hos. 5:13 ; 2 Ki. 16:5–9). But the warrior king of Assyria "cannot cure you, nor heal you of your wound" (v. 13). No political power could heal Ephraim of its fatal sickness of sin. As a nation, it was doomed to destruction and death.

The great Assyrian empire was powerless to help because God had already determined to destroy Israel: "For I will be like a lion to Ephraim, and like a young lion to the house of Judah. I, even I, will tear them and go away; I will take them away, and no one shall rescue" (v. 14). Because Israel and Judah had looked to powerless political potentates for help, God would no longer work slowly and silently to destroy them. Instead, the Lord announced that He Himself would attack and destroy these nations through the use of foreign powers like Assyria and Babylon. Like a lion, God would tear them to pieces and carry them away to the dens of their oppressors.

And as a lion returns to his den after rending and devouring its prey, so the Lord said, "I will return again to My place till they acknowledge their offense. Then they will seek My face; in their affliction they will earnestly seek Me" (v. 15).

Israel is still estranged from God today. Yet God's ultimate purpose for judging Israel is restoration. He will become inaccessible and unapproachable to Israel until it does two things: (1) comes to God in humble repentance, acknowledging its sins and (2) turns away from all human help and seeks the Lord's face in prayer, crying out for His grace and mercy.

After centuries of suffering, Israel will one day earnestly seek the Lord. This will take place during the Great Tribulation when the nation will undergo the greatest suffering in its history as Satan tries to destroy it. God will rescue Israel. And afterward, Israel will experience ultimate relief from pain and be rewarded as a nation.

There is a timely lesson here for the nations of the world. Political alliances are not the answer to survival because political power is unable to bring any nation grace and prosperity. God alone can rescue a nation from affliction and destruction. And one day, He will judge every nation according to His Word.

CHAPTER 7

SUPERFICIAL REPENTANCE

A doctor once stated, "Three hundred of my patients, when notified they were dying, repented of their sins and professed faith in God. Once they were restored to health, only 10 of the 300 manifested any evidence of a changed life." This unfortunate statistic is true not only of people but of nations as well.

In Hosea 5, God pronounced judgment on Israel. He sentenced Ephraim to be consumed slowly and silently like a woolen garment eaten by a moth. God also said He would allow Israel to be torn in pieces and carried away to the dens of her oppressors. However, it has always been God's purpose to use judgment not to destroy Israel but, rather, to bring the nation to repentance. In judgment, God leaves the door of His grace open, providing the opportunity to return to Him in sincerity.

Israel's Immediate Response

Sensing its hopeless condition, Israel cried out, "Come, and let us return to the LORD; for He has torn, but He will heal us; He has stricken, but he will bind us up" (Hos. 6:1). The people realized that if they were to survive, only God, the Great Physician, could heal their deadly wound (Ex. 15:26; Dt. 32:39). The Israelites appeared to be coming before the Lord in true repentance; but in actuality, they did not. Theirs was a superficial repentance. The text gives no indication that they ever confessed wrongdoing or turned away from practicing paganism, immorality, and murder. Their words lacked sincerity, as evidenced by their unchanged lifestyle.

Israel was confident of swift restoration once it returned to

God: "After two days will He revive us; on the third day He will raise us up, that we may live in His sight" (Hos. 6:2). The phrase *two days . . . on the third* day is a Hebrew idiom that refers to an expected swift and certain recovery from judgment. Some interpreters spiritualize it to refer to Christ's resurrection after being three days in the grave. However, this interpretation is totally foreign to the context of the passage. Others teach that God's wrath will be short and temporary, then Israel will be swiftly restored. This scenario is not the case either; the northern kingdom is yet to be restored as a nation. Another view teaches that this phrase speaks of the reestablishment of the Jewish people in their land following the Babylonian Captivity. This explanation also is unlikely because the verse refers to a specific time when the northern tribes of Israel are restored to the land. The Bible teaches that the Assyrians destroyed Israel (2 Ki. 17:4–23); it would be many centuries before Israel would be revived and raised up (Hos. 3:4–5).

Still others teach that the phrase *after two days will He revive us* means that after 2,000 years (a day being as a thousand years and a thousand years as a day, 2 Pet. 3:8), at Christ's Second Coming, Israel will be given spiritual life. They teach that the words *on the third day He will raise us up* refer to the 12 tribes being restored to the land at the beginning of Christ's 1,000-year reign on Earth. While it is true that at Christ's Second Coming, Israel will be revived to spiritual life, raised up as a nation, and replanted in its land, the argument is nevertheless flawed (Ezek. 37:12–25). The destruction of Israel mentioned in Hosea refers not to the Roman destruction 2,000 years ago but to the Assyrian destruction more than 2,700 years ago. Hosea 6:2 has nothing to do with a 2,000-year time period but simply sets forth Israel's expectation of being swiftly restored to its former state once it returned to God.

The Israelites had a shallow concept of spiritual renewal. They thought God would restore them if they simply acknowledged His presence and preeminence: "Let us know, let us pursue the knowledge of the LORD. His going forth is established as the morning; He will come to us like the rain, like the latter and former rain to the earth" (Hos. 6:3). In other words, as assuredly as the morning sun burns away the gloom of darkness and the water brings life to parched ground, so Israel believed that by acknowledging God, it would experience spiritual renewal and restoration. Again, these were empty words. God requires true repentance that involves contrition of heart, confession, forsaking of sin, and a change in conduct.

Israel's Insincere Repentance

Thus the Lord, who knows the hearts of all men, asked Israel and Judah a rhetorical question: "O Ephraim, what shall I do to you? O Judah, what shall I do to you? For your faithfulness is like a morning cloud, and like the early dew it goes away" (v. 4). God had tried everything to woo Israel and Judah away from their idolatry and bring them to repentance and commitment to Him, but His attempts were futile. If severe punishment did not bring them to repentance, what more could be done? God asked the question to draw Israel's attention to its lack of love and piety toward Him. Its faithfulness was like a morning cloud that does not deliver rain and like the drops of early morning dew that promise refreshment but dry up in the rising sun. Such "faithfulness" was neither consistent nor permanent but superficial and fleeting.

Hosea reminded Israel and Judah of the process God used to bring judgment on them: "Therefore I have hewn them by the prophets, I have slain them by the words of My mouth; and your judgments are like light that goes forth" (v. 5). God used the prophets' words as a knife to whittle away at the immoral practices of Israel and Judah, hoping to shape them according to His will as one sculpts wood. Since the prophets' words brought neither nation to repentance, however, God spoke. And His judgment fell on them like a flash of lightning.

Hosea warned Israel and Judah that God cannot be propitiated by a multitude of sacrifices and offerings. Presented without love of God and sincere holiness, they are unacceptable to Him: "For I desire mercy [loyal love] and not sacrifice, and the knowledge of God more than burnt offerings" (v. 6). Pleasing God can only be accomplished by knowing Him personally and ordering our conduct according to His will. The Israelites were unable to experience or express this kind of commitment to God because they had lost their knowledge of Him. After King Saul had transgressed against God, Samuel told him,

Has the LORD as great delight in burnt offerings and sacrifices, as in obeying the voice of the LORD? Behold, to obey is better than sacrifice, and to heed than the fat of rams. For rebellion is as the sin of witchcraft, and stubbornness is as iniquity and idolatry (1 Sam. 15:22–23).

Soulless sacrifice offered by men steeped in sin was and is, even today, an abomination to God.

Israel's Immoral Rebellion

In the following verses, God provides a number of similes and metaphors to illustrate ancient Israel's gross paganism, immorality, and murderous actions.

ADAM. First, the Lord said, "But like men [literally, "Adam"] they transgressed the covenant; there they dealt treacherously with Me" (Hos. 6:7). Some believe that the word *Adam* refers to the man Adam. In the Edenic Covenant, God set forth the blessings Adam would receive by obediently following Him. But in the Adamic Covenant, He set forth the conditions of life that fallen man must now endure until the Kingdom Age (Gen. 3:15–19). Like Adam, Israel forfeited the blessings of its covenant relationship by disobeying God.

Other commentators, however, believe that the word *Adam* refers to a city of the same name—a town close to Jordan (beside Zarethan), near the mouth of the Jabbok River and 18 miles above Jericho. It was here where the waters miraculously parted as the Israelites crossed the Jordan River (Josh. 3:16–17). The phrase *there they dealt treacherously [deceitfully] with Me* could apply to Adam and Eve in the Garden of Eden or to Israel at the city of Adam. Commentators disagree on the meaning of this verse.

GILEAD. The second illustration refers to the city of Gilead: "Gilead is a city of evildoers and defiled [tracked] with blood" (Hos. 6:8). Gilead is a mountain region stretching about 60 miles long and 20 miles wide, bordered on the north by Bashan and on the south by Moab and Ammon, extending from the Sea of Galilee to the Dead Sea (Gen. 31:21, 25; Dt. 3:12–17). Hosea 6:8 probably refers not to the area of Gilead but to the city of Ramoth Gilead, which had become a rendezvous for wicked men.

Ironically, it was one of the cities of refuge (Josh. 21:38) but was now a city known for its brutal murders.

SHECHEM. The third illustration refers to Shechem, another city of refuge located between Ebal and Gerizim (Josh. 21:21). It had become an area where "bands of robbers [marauders] lie in wait [in ambush] for a man" and "the company [band] of priests murder on the way to Shechem; surely they commit lewdness" (Hos. 6:9). Shechem lay to the north of Jerusalem and was located on the main road that pilgrims used to travel to the annual feast days in Jerusalem. It was in Shechem where priests from Israel, steeped in Baal worship, waited to plunder those going to Jerusalem. If the people offered any resistance, these priests often murdered them. Furthermore, the priests committed lewdness, meaning the vilest of sexual sins—incest (Lev. 18:17), cult prostitution (Lev. 19:29), rape (Jud. 20:5–6), and adultery (Job 31:9–11).

Chapter 6 closes with God's condemnation of the northern and southern kingdoms. Speaking on behalf of the Lord, Hosea said, "I have seen a horrible thing in the house of Israel: There is the harlotry of Ephraim; Israel is defiled" (Hos. 6:10). Ephraim was the major tribe of Israel that practiced harlotry—religious prostitution connected with fertility rites found in Baal worship. This practice had spread from Ephraim throughout all Israel and eventually to Judah.

Thus Judah would not escape judgment: "Also, O Judah, a harvest is appointed for you" (v. 11). Judah had committed the same sins as Israel and would reap the same harvest. Yet destruction is not Israel's final destiny, for God said He will return "the captives of My people" (v. 11). One day God will restore both the northern and southern kingdoms. This return will come to ultimate fruition at the inception of the Millennial Kingdom (Ezek. 37:15–22).

Ancient Israel's superficial repentance should remind us that it is not enough for a wayward believer to feel sorry for his or her sin and simply say, "I will return to the Lord and He will take away my sin." This is not true repentance. True repentance takes place when we feel the awesome, convicting power of the Holy Spirit deep in our souls and realize that we have sinned against Almighty God. Truly repentant sinners will not only confess and forsake their evil ways but exhibit a turnabout in their lives and alter their conduct accordingly.

Do you, like Israel, tolerate sin in your life? If you do not deal with it, God will.

CHAPTER 8

SLIDING TOWARD ANARCHY

It is often said that a picture is worth a thousand words. Yet in chapter 7 of Hosea, the prophet's words paint a vivid picture of Israel's pursuit of immorality as the nation set aside God's law, degenerated, and slid toward anarchy and national disaster. Worse, however, than the nation's moral decline was the blindness of Israel's leaders who lacked any conscious awareness of their sin. These factors produced a spirit of anarchy and chaos within the northern kingdom during the final days before the Assyrian invasion. Little did Israel know that its days were numbered. The mighty Assyrians would soon appear and devastate the nation.

Civil Rebellion

God eagerly looked forward to bringing spiritual healing to Israel, but its recalcitrant involvement in gross immorality made such renewal impossible:

> *When I would have healed Israel, then the iniquity of Ephraim was uncovered, and the wickedness of Samaria. For they have committed fraud; a thief comes in; a band of robbers takes spoil outside* (Hos. 7:1).

Degeneracy existed everywhere; the country was filled with lying, home invasions, and street crime. Forsaking God's law had robbed the nation of its faith, honesty, integrity, and material possessions.

Israel had lost sight of the fact that God kept a record of every evil act: "They do not consider in their hearts that I remember all their wickedness; now their own deeds have surrounded them;

they are before My face" (v. 2). Israel was so consumed with wickedness and entangled in sin that it had become callous and indifferent to God's law, making it impervious to any sense of accountability before Him.

In every society, the leadership sets the standards for morality and justice. But Israel's leaders had succumbed to wickedness. Their moral corruption and depravity were like leaven, permeating the whole nation from top to bottom. In fact, the king and "princes" (military leaders) rejoiced over their people's wickedness and lies and listened with amusement to the vileness of their people's escapades (v. 3).

Using a number of similes and metaphors, Hosea vividly described the nation's wickedness. He compared its lust and immoral lack of restraint to the heating of an oven used to bake leavened bread: "They are all adulterers. Like an oven heated by a baker—he ceases stirring the fire after kneading the dough, until it is leavened" (v. 4). The baker kindled the fire in his oven the night before, and early in the morning all he needed to do was stoke it until the fire roared. When the flame died down, the oven provided an even heat. The baker would slap the flat, leavened cakes onto the oven walls, and there they would remain until the dough was completely fermented. Then he stoked the fire to an extreme temperature to bake the cakes. In like manner, Israel's passions simmered until new opportunities for immorality cropped up. Then the fire of their lust burst into flame.

Continuing the metaphor, Hosea illustrated how the lust for power had induced the princes of Israel to be wicked to their king:

> In the day of our king princes have made him sick, inflamed with wine; he stretched out his hand with scoffers. They prepare their heart like an oven, while they lie in wait; their baker sleeps all night; in the morning it burns like a flaming fire. They are all hot, like an oven, and have devoured their judges; all their kings have fallen. None among them calls upon Me (vv. 5–7).

The celebration described was either the king's birthday or recognition of his coronation day. The prevailing strategy was to get the king and his court so intoxicated that they became sick with wine and completely incapacitated. Subversive princes who were invited to feast with their king burned like a heated oven in their lust to assassinate him. These conspirators waited through the night in anger. In the morning, they ignited their plot and slew him. Then they took over his throne and established their own rule.

Nineteen kings ruled over the northern kingdom of Israel. Some died natural deaths, but the majority were dethroned or murdered. Zechariah, Shallum, Pekahiah, and Pekah were all murdered in office. Menahem became a vassal to the Assyrians, who imprisoned Hoshea, Israel's last king. Ironically, through this entire scenario, "none among them calls upon Me," said the Lord (v. 7). No one called on God to bring stability in Israel as it slid into anarchy.

Chastisement Revealed

God had instructed Israel to remain separate from the surrounding nations (Num. 23:9; Dt. 33:28). However, the 10 tribes assimilated themselves and their religion into the heathen nations that dwelt nearby. Hosea described this amalgamation as a half-baked cake: "Ephraim has mixed himself among the peoples; Ephraim is a cake unturned" (Hos. 7:8). In biblical times people baked bread on hot rocks. If they did not turn the bread continually, it would burn to a crisp on one side but remain uncooked on the other side. Israel's intermingling with the Gentile nations left it burned politically and religiously; but in its commitment to the Lord, it remained "uncooked." A half-baked cake is good for nothing and must be discarded. So it was with Israel.

This sorry state left Israel like an old man who is weak and susceptible to abuse but who proudly refuses to acknowledge it. Hosea put it well: "Aliens have devoured his strength, but he does not know it; yes, gray hairs are here and there on him, yet he does not know it" (v. 9). Like an old man, Israel bore all the marks of impending death. Its spiritual strength had been diminished by idolatry and its wealth depleted by paying tribute to Assyria. And like an old man unaware of his condition, Israel was blind to its decaying state.

What's more, "The pride of Israel testifies to his face, but they do not return to the LORD their God, nor seek Him for all this" (v. 10). God got right in Israel's face and testified against its immorality, idolatry, and insensitivity toward Him and His Word. Sadly, this rebuke still did not bring the backsliding nation to repent or reverse its position.

Although deteriorating, Israel—like "a silly dove, without sense"—pursued protective alliances with Egypt and Assyria (v. 11). When attacked, a harmless dove will flitter back and forth, confused about what to do to ward off danger. The dove is "without sense," meaning she lacks the ability to make a rational choice regarding the correct action to take. Like the dove, Israel lacked the ability to make a rational choice. Instead of calling on God for assistance, it irrationally called on heathen nations for help.

While Israel flittered back and forth, making alliances with Assyria and Egypt, God intervened in judgment:

> Wherever they go, I will spread My net on them; I will bring them down like birds of the air; I will chastise them according to what their congregation has heard (v. 12).

Metaphorically, God would come with a fowler's net, waiting to catch the silly dove of Israel as it flew back and forth in confusion. Israel would not escape judgment. At the right time, God would use the Assyrians to net the nation and carry it into captivity. Israel had received ample warning that its captivity was imminent if repentance was not forthcoming.

The threat of judgment was followed by the Lord's announcement of destruction:

> Woe to them, for they have fled from Me! Destruction to them, because they have transgressed against Me! Though I redeemed them, yet they have spoken lies against Me (v. 13).

In the past, God had delivered Israel from Egypt and other oppressors bent on its destruction. He was still ready to deliver Israel if the nation would only call on Him for help. Instead, it looked to other nations to deliver it from danger. Even worse, Israelites had lied about God's ability, power, and willingness to protect them. Thus God said, "Destruction to them!"

During the reign of King Menahem (752–742 B.C.), the

Assyrians, led by Tiglath-Pileser III, began moving west to enlarge their holdings. In the process, they threatened the northern kingdom. Menahem knuckled under to the demands of Tiglath-Pileser and paid enormous tribute to the Assyrian leader. Later, Israel's King Pekah joined Syria with plans to plunder Judah. At Judah's request, Assyria intervened on Judah's behalf, and Tiglath-Pileser seized the northern kingdom of Israel in 733 B.C.

When the Assyrians invaded Israel, they destroyed the crops used for food and drink. In the midst of its calamity, Israel "did not cry out to Me with their heart when they wailed upon their beds. They assemble together for grain and new wine, they rebel against Me," said the Lord (v. 14).

The Israelites approached the living God in the same manner they approached Baal. They howled over the loss of their crops and tried to persuade God to help them by cutting themselves, as did Baal worshipers (1 Ki. 18:28)—something strictly prohibited by the Mosaic Law (Dt. 14:1).

In His goodness, God had "disciplined and strengthened their arms" during their time of need; but He received no gratitude (Hos. 7:15). In fact, He said, "they devise evil against Me" (v. 15). In disloyalty, Israel treated God as the enemy and plotted the worst kind of evil against Him. Israel's extreme hostility is all the more horrifying when compared to God's loving grace and mercy expressed in verse 15.

Finally, Israel's backsliding and unbelief are compared to a defective bow:

> *They return, but not to the Most High; they are like a treacherous bow. Their princes shall fall by the sword for the cursings of their tongue. This shall be their derision in the land of Egypt* (v. 16).

Israel took confidence in its ability to defeat its enemies and therefore did not seek God's help. But its confidence was like a defective bow; when used in battle, it either broke or could not shoot an arrow with power and accuracy. As a result of the nation's insolence, Israel's princes fell by the sword. Even the Egyptians, whom Israel had called on for help, scorned the nation when they heard of its defeat.

When Tiglath-Pileser finally captured Israel, he set up

Hoshea as king in Samaria. Hoshea acknowledged Assyrian rule for a time but eventually stopped paying tribute and sought an alliance with Egypt in an attempt to overthrow Assyria's control. This rebellion led to a three-year siege by the Assyrians, ending with the captivity of the northern kingdom in 722 B.C. (2 Ki. 17:3–4).

As it was with the Israelites, the moral compass of many Christians today is off course. We, too, need to reexamine our commitment to the Lord and make the needed adjustments while there is still time.

CHAPTER 9

WINDS OF JUDGMENT

Few things are more destructive than a tornado. Its funnel-shaped wind can swirl up to 500 miles per hour, devastating everything in its path. The mere sight of the cloud is usually terrifying, and most people who have experienced tornadoes know these great twisters leave little time to prepare and few places to hide. In chapter 8, Hosea revealed that God's judgment is like a tornado. Israel's idolatry and immorality would bring judgment that would sweep the nation, destroying everything in its path.

Predicted Invasion

God had stationed Hosea as a faithful watchman over Israel to warn of impending judgment. He commanded Hosea,

Set the trumpet to your mouth! He shall come like an eagle against the house of the LORD, because they have transgressed My covenant and rebelled against My law (Hos. 8:1).

The phrase *house of the LORD* refers not to the Temple in Jerusalem but to the northern tribes of Israel. Today cities have sirens to warn of a tornado or invasion. In biblical times, Israel blew a trumpet to signal that danger was near.

Hosea alerted Israel to prepare for an invasion from the mighty Assyrian army. Soon the Assyrians would swoop down on Israel like eagles snatching their prey. This image aptly symbolizes the Assyrians because their attacks were swift and brutal. God had raised up Assyria to judge Israel, directly fulfilling Moses' prophecy: "The LORD will bring a nation against you from afar, from the end of the earth, as swift as the eagle flies" (Dt. 28:49). Israel had transgressed God's covenant and His law (Hos. 8:1). This verse reiterates God's first indictment against Israel (6:7). In the preceding seven chapters, Hosea detailed how Israel had committed gross and abominable sins. Although the nation had numerous opportunities to repent, it continued to sin and rebel against God's love and mercy.

Hearing of judgment, Israel hypocritically cried, "My God, we know You!" (v. 2). The nation's appeal was twofold: First, Israel claimed to be God's people. Second, it claimed to know God. The nation was saying, "We are your people, God. So deliver us from the coming judgment." Yet Israel's immorality and idolatry proved, in fact, that it neither knew the Lord nor desired to practice His law (4:1, 6; 5:4).

So God ignored Israel's plea for help. The nation had "rejected the good; the enemy will pursue him" (v. 3). Israel had rejected God's goodness, mercy, and love. Consequently, God would not hear the nation's plea. The Assyrian invasion was inevitable.

Pronouncement of Iniquity

CIVIL REBELLION. At this point, Hosea listed the indictments against Israel that precipitated God's judgment. First, Israel had committed civil rebellion.

They set up kings, but not by Me; they made princes, but I did not acknowledge them. From their silver and gold they made idols for themselves—that they might be cut off (v. 4).

Even in its revolt against King Rehoboam, Solomon's son, Israel had failed to seek God's guidance or approval. Ten tribes split from the southern kingdom of Judah without consulting Him. During the divided-kingdom period, not one of Israel's kings was chosen by the will of God. Men in Israel schemed, slew their rivals, and set up rulers and princes whom God never approved.

CORRUPT RELIGIOUS SYSTEM. Second, Israel had installed a corrupt religious system. It amassed gold and silver to construct golden calves and silver idols in Bethel and Dan and instituted Baal worship in direct violation of the second commandment (Ex. 20:4). The degrading, idolatrous practice offended God from start to finish and denied His sovereignty over Israel.

Jeroboam I had established calf worship at Dan and Bethel, misleading the people to assume that God accepted such worship (1 Ki. 12:28–31). God vented His anger: "Your calf is rejected, O Samaria! My anger is aroused against them—how long until they attain to innocence?" (Hos. 8:5). No evidence exists of calf worship in Samaria, Israel's capital. Nevertheless, Hosea linked calf worship in Bethel to the citizens of Samaria (10:5–6). The statement "Your calf is rejected, O Samaria" is better translated, "He [God] has rejected your calf, O Samaria." Israel had rejected what was good and had turned to idols, so the Lord responded by rejecting Israel's idols.

God's anger burned against Israel's idolatry. He asked how long it would be until the Israelites "attain[ed] to innocence." That is, when would the nation be cleansed from idolatry and become pure in God's eyes? The question is really God's lament concerning Israel's impurity. Idolatry was so deeply embedded in the fabric of Israel's culture that one wondered whether the nation would ever overcome the sin. It took the destruction and captivity of both Judah and Israel to finally break the nation of idolatry.

Concerning the construction of an idol, Hosea said, "A workman made it, and it is not God; but the calf of Samaria shall be broken to pieces" (8:6). Israel was without excuse concerning idols, for everyone knew idols were man-made, not divine, and eventually would be smashed to pieces.

Hosea used a metaphor of cause and effect to express the futility and emptiness of Israel's idolatrous practices and the foolishness of its foreign policy: "They sow the wind, and reap the whirlwind" (v. 7). Wind symbolizes futility and fickleness, which often turn into a whirlwind that brings destruction. Israel's idolatry and foreign policy would bring a whirlwind of destruction from the Assyrian army.

Hosea continued with the sowing metaphor: "The stalk has no bud; it shall never produce meal. If it should produce, aliens would swallow it up" (v. 7). Perhaps the seed would sprout, but it would not produce an ear of corn to make meal. Moreover, even if a plant did produce grain, Israel's labor would still be in vain because the nation's enemy would seize the grain for itself.

COMPROMISING RELATIONSHIP. Israel had entered a compromising relationship with Assyria and Egypt. Hosea said, "Israel is swallowed up; now they are among the Gentiles like a vessel in which is no pleasure" (v. 8). Assyria swallowed up Israel in 722 B.C., turning it into a province, sapping its power, and draining its prosperity by requiring the nation to pay tribute. Neighboring nations considered Israel nothing but a cheap, worthless clay pot to be cast aside.

Hosea compared Israel's alliance with Assyria to that of a wild donkey and a prostitute: "For they have gone up to Assyria, like a wild donkey alone by itself; Ephraim has hired lovers" (v. 9). In its stubborn self-will and independence, Israel embarked on a solitary course to carve out its destiny without consulting God. Instead of being faithful to God (Israel's "Husband"), the nation prostituted itself to the Gentiles by bribing the heathen Assyrians. In return, Israel hoped to maintain its political power and prestige and expected Assyria to protect it from God's judgment. Usually a prostitute receives payment for her services, but Israel was so unwanted that it had to pay Assyria.

All of Israel's attempts to protect itself from God's punishment were futile. God said, "Yes, though they have hired among the nations, now I will gather them; and they shall sorrow a little, because of the burden of the king of princes" (v. 10).

God cut off all help Israel had sought from Assyria and Egypt and hemmed the nation in for judgment. The Israelites would sorrow because of the financial tribute they were required to pay to Assyria; but such tribute would be nothing compared to the judgment from God. Ironically, God used "the king of princes" (Assyria)—the very nation from whom Israel sought help—as His rod of correction.

Indeed, God's punishment was justified because Israel had erected many altars to idols, particularly to the Canaanite fertility deity, Baal. The altars Ephraim erected were "altars for sin" (v. 11). With every altar it built, Israel multiplied its sin, plunging the nation deeper and deeper into iniquity and guilt.

People's Indifference

Israel was without excuse. God said, "I have written for him the great things of My law, but they were considered a strange thing" (v. 12). The Israelites had the ceremonial, civil, and moral law that revealed how to walk before the Lord. The Law included numerous directions, precepts, and prohibitions that were so explicit, comprehensive, and minute that Israel could not help but know what God demanded in true worship. Yet they treated the Law like an alien that had no place in their thoughts.

The priests sacrificed throughout the land, not to please God or expiate sin, but selfishly, to acquire personal gain. Such practices offended God, and He totally rejected them. Hosea said, "But the LORD does not accept them. Now He will remember their iniquity and punish their sins. They shall return to Egypt" (v. 13). The cup of Israel's iniquity was full, and the hour of its judgment had come. The word *Egypt* symbolizes exile, bondage, slavery, oppression, toil, and sorrow. The Israelites, of course, would not literally return to Egypt. But they would suffer the same plight and conditions they experienced in Egypt before their deliverance under Moses. Egypt represents the new exile and bondage Israel would endure under Assyria.

Hosea stated both the nature of Israel and Judah's sin and the source of their suffering:

> For Israel has forgotten his Maker, and has built temples; Judah also has multiplied fortified cities; but I will send fire upon his cities, and it shall devour his palaces (v. 14).

God was Israel's salvation and security. How could the nation forget its Maker? Moreover, Moses had clearly warned that if Israel forgot God, it would perish (Dt. 8:19). Israel became known as "the land of forgetfulness" (Ps. 88:12). In like manner, Judah also became infected with forgetfulness of God's grace. Judah hoped its fortified cities would bring security from its enemies. Fortified cities symbolize a futile turning from trust in God to trust in one's self-sufficiency. God promised to devour Judah's cities and palaces, and He did so in part when He used Sennacherib of Assyria to destroy all of Judah's fortified cities except Jerusalem. Thus Israel experienced the fulfillment of what it was promised if the nation forgot God (Dt. 28:52).

Thousands of years later, Hosea still has a lesson for us today. Israel had not forgotten God intellectually but had neglected God spiritually. Its self-sufficient attitude resulted in national indifference, immorality, and idolatry. We, too, must remember that we not only reap what we sow, but we often reap more than we sow. And though the harvest may not come immediately, its arrival is inevitable.

CHAPTER 10

A NATION'S FATE

One of the greatest paintings of all time is Michelangelo's *The Last Judgment.* The entire work, painted on the altar wall of the Sistine Chapel, reflects the despair of people who are marked for judgment. Though some elements of the painting may be unbiblical, its message reminds us, nevertheless, that God will surely judge those who have rejected His saving grace for a life of sin.

When the 16th-century painting was unveiled, a storm of conviction is said to have fallen on the viewers. Later, all Europe reportedly trembled as the work was explained from city to city through pictures.

Hosea also painted a portrait of sorts. His words vividly depicted Israel's sinful condition. But, unlike the people who saw *The Last Judgment,* the Israelites neither repented nor trembled at the message. Instead, they seemed to live in disbelief that judgment would soon destroy them. In chapter 9, God condemns Israel's degrading practices, which resulted in the withdrawal of His presence and the announcement of the nation's demise.

Captivity Declared

Hosea sternly reprimanded Israel for making the Feast of Tabernacles pagan: "Do not rejoice, O Israel, with joy like other peoples; for you have played the harlot against your God. You have made love for hire on every threshing floor" (Hos. 9:1). During the Feast of Tabernacles, Israel attributed its plentiful harvest not to God but to Baal and participated in the licentiousness linked to Baal worship. Prostitutes frequented the threshing floors and winepresses to commit adultery with the men who guarded the grain. These sins involved wild shouting and merrymaking that degraded the character of the Feast. Israel's immorality and idolatry would result in God removing future harvests: "The threshing floor and the winepress shall not feed them, and the new wine shall fail in her" (v. 2). This judgment was a direct fulfillment of Moses' prophecy before Israel entered the land (Dt. 28:38–42, 51).

Hosea prophesied, "They shall not dwell in the LORD's land, but Ephraim shall return to Egypt, and shall eat unclean things in Assyria" (Hos. 9:3). The Israelites would not literally return to Egypt but would suffer the same conditions of exile, bondage, slavery, oppression, toil, and sorrow that they experienced there. However, they would be exiled to Assyria, where they would be forced to eat "unclean things." They had dedicated their harvest to Baal; therefore, the Lord would remove their kosher, sanctified food and make them eat unclean food that had been offered to idols. Israel would dwell in the defiled country of Assyria without a sanctuary, sacrifice, or sanctified food.

During the Assyrian captivity, all their means of worship according to the Levitical Law would be cut off. The wine offerings would cease; and should Israel attempt to offer sacrifices in Assyria, such sacrifices would "be like bread of mourners to them; all who eat it shall be defiled [polluted]. For their bread shall. . . not come into the house of the LORD" (v. 4). God vowed that eating such sacrifices would bring no joy or satisfaction. Instead, they would be like the unclean bread of mourners. Everything mourners touched became unclean because they had touched a dead body (Num. 19:14–15, 22). Mourners' bread was unclean and unfit to use for worship. Therefore, all who ate of the sacrifice would become polluted as well.

Hosea proceeded to ask Israel a rhetorical question concerning its ability to celebrate the feast in exile: "What will you do in the appointed day, and in the day of the feast of the LORD?" (Hos. 9:5). Naturally, Israel's religious calendar ceased to have significance during the nation's captivity in Assyria. In exile it would be unable to worship. One can only imagine the condemnation the Israelites felt when their feast days arrived. Eventually, Israel's spiritual life diminished.

Hosea envisioned the great destruction that was soon to fall on Israel. The prophet knew that those who escaped death and captivity during the Assyrian siege would flee to Egypt for refuge. Hosea revealed that "Egypt shall gather them up; Memphis shall bury them" (v. 6). That is, despite their escape to Egypt, they would still experience death and be buried in Memphis. Memphis was the ancient capital of Egypt on the western bank of the Nile, south of old Cairo, where Egypt buried its kings. It was, in fact, in Memphis where the Egyptians buried the Israelites who died. The Israelites who returned to Israel after the siege found only wasted cities. Hosea prophesied, "Nettles shall possess their valuables of silver; thorns shall be in their tents" (v. 6). All their precious possessions of silver (including idols) were confiscated; their cities, homes, and places of worship became overgrown with weeds, thorns, and thistles.

Corruption Denounced

Again Hosea enumerated the reasons for judgment. First, he said, "The prophet is a fool, the spiritual man is insane" (v. 7). Some believe this prophecy expresses the people's response to Hosea and his ministry. Others believe it is Hosea's condemnation of Israel's false prophets. Commentators marshal strong arguments for both interpretations. However, the context would indicate that it is Hosea's prophecy against the false prophets of Israel. The word *fool* means "insane," and the word *spiritual* can be interpreted "wind." Thus the phrase says that the words of a false prophet lack substance and are like the wind. Such a one is mad or insane. Second, Hosea said a false prophet is filled with "iniquity, and great enmity [hatred]" (v. 7). The people harbored extreme bitterness toward Hosea for denouncing their sins and prophets. Their bitterness stirred them to hostility and to hold grudges against Hosea and God.

In contrast to Israel's false prophets, Hosea said, "The watchman of Ephraim is with my God" (v. 8). Some believe Ephraim is being identified as God's watchman. But the watchman is Hosea, not Ephraim. Hosea claimed to be the watchman with God, standing on the watchtower and faithfully predicting the nation's coming judgment. To this statement, the people said, "But the prophet is a fowler's snare in all his ways—enmity in the house of his God" (v. 8). Thus Israel, called "the house of God," treated Hosea like a wild beast and continually set a trap in hopes of killing him.

God compares Ephraim's sin to the brutal gang rape and murder of a Levite's concubine at Gibeah. "They are deeply corrupted, as in the days of Gibeah" (v. 9). This sin was considered the worst act committed since Israel left Egypt (Jud. 19:30). Hosea claimed that Israel's profound injustices against God and him fell into the same category as the sin in Gibeah. God did not forget to bring judgment in that instance; nor would He forget now.

Hosea's announcement of judgment is then interrupted with a flashback. God recalls Israel's early history and reflects on the sadness He felt over what the Israelites had become.

I found Israel like grapes in the wilderness; I saw your fathers as the firstfruits on the fig tree in its first season. But they went to Baal Peor, and separated themselves to that shame; they became an abomination like the thing they loved (Hos. 9:10).

God compares His joy over Israel to that of a weary traveler who finds grapes growing in the desert—which is totally unlikely. The fathers of the nation were compared to the first ripened figs, the sweetest of all fruit. These metaphors express God's delight over Israel and His intent to do great things through the nation. But Israel abused its privileged relationship with God and pursued the shameful practices of idolatry, described as an abomination.

Children Denied

Israel believed that by practicing pagan fertility rites, it would be guaranteed many children and bountiful crops. But God said,

As for Ephraim, their glory shall fly away like a bird—No birth, no pregnancy, and no conception! Though they bring up their children, yet I will bereave them to the last man. . . . Ephraim is stricken, their root is dried up; they shall bear no fruit. Yes, were they to bear children, I would kill the darlings of their womb (vv. 11–12, 16).

Israel would lose its prosperity and become barren and

sterile as quickly as a bird takes flight. Although it was a vibrant, fruitful land, it would become desolate. Though the women would conceive, their children would die through miscarriages, accidents, and disease.

Hosea compared Ephraim's fate to that of Tyre: "I saw Ephraim like Tyre, planted in a pleasant place, so Ephraim will bring out his children to the murderer" (v. 13). God had wanted Israel to become prosperous like the city of Tyre; but like Tyre, immorality and idolatry became its downfall. God would destroy Israel as He did Tyre, and Israel's children would be murdered during the Assyrian invasion.

Knowing judgment was coming, Hosea prayed that God would withhold children from Israel. "Give them, O LORD—what will You give? Give them a miscarrying womb and dry breasts!" (v. 14). This God did.

Coming Dispersion

God's tone toward Israel now turns angry:

All their wickedness is in Gilgal, for there I hated them. Because of the evil of their deeds I will drive them from My house; I will love them no more. All their princes are rebellious (v. 15).

It was in Gilgal where Israel practiced immorality and idolatry like an adulterous wife. In anger, God removed His protective care from the nation and drove it from His "house" (the land of Israel). There was no "prince" (leader) in Israel to guide the nation back to God; the leaders had all rebelled against Him.

Israel's fate was sealed: "My God will cast them away, because they did not obey Him; and they shall be wanderers among the nations" (v. 17). God would temporarily cast Israel out of its land and make the Jewish people wander throughout the world for centuries. This 2,700-year-old prophecy foretells what we call today the Diaspora—the Jewish dispersion. It explains why the Jewish people are scattered around the globe and why they struggle to return to the land that rightfully belongs to them. What a great price this nation has paid for its infidelity.

CHAPTER 11

THE WAGES OF SIN

Sin is like a moral cancer, infecting everything it touches. If you do not deal with it, it will corrupt you. What is true of moral corruption in man is also true in nations. When God confronted Israel about its spiritual and moral malignancy, the nation refused to deal with it. In chapter 10, Hosea traced the pattern of sin that ultimately resulted in the nation's demise.

Sin Addressed

Hosea spoke of Israel's sin in agricultural terms, describing the nation as an empty vine:

> *Israel empties his vine; he brings forth fruit for himself. According to the multitude of his fruit he has increased the altars; according to the bounty of his land they have embellished his sacred pillars [handsome images]* (Hos. 10:1).

The word *empty* in Hebrew means "luxuriant" and refers to the overflowing abundance of fruit Israel enjoyed during the days of Jeroboam II (793–753 B.C.). But because the Israelites attributed their prosperity to the false gods of Baal rather than to Jehovah, the more they prospered, the more extensive and elaborate became the idols they made.

Hosea called Israel double-minded: "Their heart is divided; now they are held guilty. He will break down their altars; He will ruin their sacred pillars [images]" (v. 2). The word *divided* means "smooth, tricky, treacherous, slippery, deceitful, unreliable speech." Israel's speech and approach to God were hypocritical, divided, and deceitful. The Israelites tried to worship both

God and Baal. Ultimately, this dual allegiance provoked God to destroy Israel's altars, images, and false religious system.

In verse 3, the Israelites realized no one could deliver them in time of war: "We have no king, because we did not fear the LORD. And as for a king, what would he do for us?" They knew that not even a king would be able to rescue them from judgment. The Assyrian invasion destroyed Israel's political power and removed its king. Afterward, Israel realized that its lack of reverential faithfulness to God caused Him to mete out judgment.

Lack of faithfulness to God also spilled over to a lack of regard for individual rights. The Israelites and their kings made legal agreements with no intention of honoring them: "They have spoken words, swearing falsely in making a covenant. Thus judgment springs up like hemlock in the furrows of the field" (v. 4). Verbal duplicity in regulating citizens' rights produced a breakdown in justice. Lawsuits sprung up quickly and plentifully, like hemlock (a poisonous herb) that grows in a fallow field.

Israel knew that judgment was imminent and feared the loss of its calf-idol:

> The inhabitants of Samaria fear because of the calf of Beth Aven. For its people mourn for it, and its priests shriek for it—because its glory has departed from it. The idol also shall be carried to Assyria as a present for King Jareb. Ephraim shall receive shame, and Israel shall be ashamed of his own counsel (vv. 5–6).

It was customary for a conquering army to carry off the gods of its defeated foe, thereby demonstrating the strength and superiority of its own gods. The idols would be melted down and presented as a gift to King Jareb. No record exists of an Assyrian king named Jareb. The phrase King Jareb means "warrior king" and is a figurative title for the king of Assyria who was the northern kingdom's final subjugator. Israel was disgraced and put to shame because it trusted in idols that were powerless to protect it in time of war (v. 6).

Assyria showed no mercy to Israel. The Assyrians stripped the land of everything:

> As for Samaria, her king is cut off like a twig [splinter of wood] on the water. Also the high places of Aven, the sin of Israel, shall be destroyed. The thorn and thistle grow on their altars (vv. 7–8).

Samaria's king was swiftly carried away like a splinter of wood on a tumultuous sea. Everything was destroyed and removed: idols, high places, and the wicked monarch. Thorns and thistles grew up, covering the site where the shrines and altars once stood. When Israel had entered Canaan, the Lord commanded the nation to destroy idolatrous sites of worship (Num. 33:52; Dt. 12:2–3); but Israel failed to obey the Lord's command. So God used a foreign army to destroy idolatry in Canaan.

In despair and anguish, the Israelites cried for the mountains and hills to cover them (Hos. 10:8). They preferred death to being captured by Assyria. Yet God did not answer Israel's cry. Unbelievers will make a similar plea when they experience the terror of God's wrath during the future Tribulation (Rev. 6:16).

Israel's sin is compared to that of Gibeah: "O Israel, you have sinned from the days of Gibeah; there they stood. The battle in Gibeah against the children of iniquity did not overtake them" (Hos. 10:9). In the days of the judges, Israel almost destroyed the entire tribe of Benjamin for sheltering the wicked men of Gibeah who brutally raped a Levite's concubine (Jud. 20:1–8). Israel experienced the same fate when the Assyrians invaded the country.

God said, "When it is My desire, I will chasten them. Peoples shall be gathered against them when I bind them for their two transgressions" (Hos. 10:10). God determined when He would punish Israel for its sin. The meaning of the phrase *when I bind them for their two transgressions* is difficult to interpret. Some believe it refers to Judah and Israel yoked together in evil (like plowing oxen) before God's eyes. Others interpret it to mean Israel is yoked to the two golden calves in Dan and Bethel. Still others believe the phrase refers to Israel's former sin at Gibeah and the priests' idolatry. Whichever view one holds, judgment on Israel was certain.

Ephraim (Israel), which was deprived of its calf-idol, is compared to a heifer: "Ephraim is a trained heifer that loves to thresh grain; but I harnessed her fair neck, I will make Ephraim pull a plow. Judah shall plow; Jacob shall break his clods" (v. 11). A young cow was trained to do easy work and allowed to be unmuzzled, so she could eat while threshing grain. In like manner, Israel lived in a comfortable land of plenty, able to indulge itself because of the prosperity God provided. Ephraim, however, failed to appreciate its situation under God's covenant relationship and became yoked to immorality and idolatry. Therefore, God would place Israel under a harsh yoke that would chafe its fair neck. Both Israel and Judah would be yoked to their enemies and forced to perform harsh labor. Plowing and harrowing were backbreaking tasks in a land like Israel with rocky, thin soil. This prophecy was fulfilled when the Assyrians destroyed Israel (722 B.C.) and Babylon took Judah captive (586 B.C.).

Salvation Available

Although destruction hung over Israel, God still announced that judgment could be averted: "Sow for yourselves righteousness; reap in mercy; break up your fallow ground, for it is time to seek the LORD, till He comes and rains righteousness on you" (v. 12). Fallow ground is land that has been plowed but left unseeded. During the growing season, it becomes hard and full of weeds. If Israel broke up the fallow ground of its hard heart, it would receive loving-kindness and mercy from God. But first, Israel needed to root out the noxious growth of sin that had overtaken it. Then it needed to seek the Lord earnestly and zealously, in true repentance. If Israel had responded in such a manner, God would have withheld judgment and would have rained righteousness on the nation.

To reinforce the need for sowing righteousness by repenting, Hosea reminded Israel of all the evil it had plowed:

You have plowed wickedness; you have reaped iniquity. You have eaten the fruit of lies, because you trusted in your own way, in the multitude of your mighty men (v. 13).

But Hosea's enumeration of Israel's sin did not bring conviction. Neither did his call to repentance. Instead, Israel turned a deaf ear to the prophet.

Sentence Announced

Because Israel failed to respond to Hosea's call to seek the Lord, the prophet had no choice but to pronounce judgment:

Therefore tumult shall arise among your people, and all your fortresses shall be plundered as Shalman plundered Beth Arbel in the day of battle—a mother dashed in pieces upon her children (v. 14).

In the siege, people could hear the noise of war and confusion. All of Israel's strongholds would be laid waste. The inhuman cruelty of the Assyrian army would be unleashed, and no one would be spared. Mothers would bend over their children to protect them, but to no avail; both would be slaughtered.

Israel's destruction is compared to Shalman's devastation of Beth Arbel. Little is known about Shalman or the city of Beth Arbel. Many scholars believe the word *Shalman* is a contracted form of *Shalmaneser,* the name of a number of Assyrian kings. Shalmaneser V, son of Tiglath-Pileser III, is the king who attacked Israel in 725 B.C. and made King Hoshea of Israel a vassal (2 Ki. 17:3).

Others believe the word *Shalman* refers to Shalamanu, a Moabite king who invaded Galilee and later paid tribute to Tiglath-Pileser. Beth Arbel may well be Arbel in Galilee. In this context, the name Shalman probably refers to Shalmaneser.

The Assyrian invasion would bring an end to Israel: "Thus it shall be done to you, O Bethel, because of your great wickedness. At dawn the king of Israel shall be cut off utterly" (Hos. 10:15). Bethel, the center of all wickedness (representing every city in Israel), would be destroyed like Beth Arbel. At dawn's light, when soldiers assemble for battle, King Hoshea would be cut off, thus ending the kingship within Israel. Israel's misplaced confidence in its military, rather than in God's power, was the nation's downfall.

Failure to deal with its spiritual malignancy resulted in Israel's inevitable judgment. God's chastisement of Israel is an example and warning to each nation in every generation that forgets God. Through the apostle Paul, God reminds us today, "Now all these things happened to them as examples, and they were written for our admonition, upon whom the ends of the ages have come" (1 Cor. 10:11).

CHAPTER 12

GOD'S LOVE FOR ISRAEL

Richard Halverson, former chaplain of the U.S. Senate, once wrote, "There is nothing you can do to make God love you more, nor is there anything you can do to make God love you less! His love is Unconditional, Impartial, Everlasting, Infinite, and Perfect." This description aptly expresses God's love for Israel.

God appears in this chapter as a loving Father grieving over Israel, His rebellious son. Israel's rebellious attitude was inexplicable in view of all that God had done for the nation. God birthed Israel; and through the centuries, He nourished, instructed, and protected the nation. But Israel proved to be an ungrateful son who insulted God by acts of immorality, idolatry, and indifference. Like any disobedient son, Israel needed chastening. So in His sovereign love, God disciplined the wayward nation in order to restore it to a loving relationship with Himself.

God's Call

From its inception as a nation, God demonstrated His love for Israel: "When Israel was a child, I loved him, and out of Egypt I called My son" (Hos. 11:1). God is pictured as a tender, loving Father who adopted Israel to be His son and entered into a covenant relationship with the nation. His choice of Israel was an act of pure, sovereign grace, not due to any merit within the nation (Dt. 7:6–8). He displayed His love by delivering Israel from 400 years of Egyptian bondage. The prophets repeatedly used this deliverance as an illustration of God's power on behalf of His people.

The phrase *and out of Egypt I called My son* also is applied typologically to Jesus Christ in Matthew 2:15. Israel, God's covenant nation, is the type; Jesus the Messiah is the antitype. Both Israel and Jesus went to Egypt for protection—Israel because of a severe famine in Canaan during the days of Joseph; Jesus because of Herod's threat to kill all children two years and under in Jerusalem and Bethlehem. Hosea's statement is a historical reference to Israel's physical redemption from Egypt. Matthew's statement refers to Jesus the Redeemer who provides spiritual redemption from the bondage of sin and eternal death.

The nation responded to God's love like a wayward son. To correct Israel's waywardness, God sent prophet after prophet to plead with the nation to repent and return to the Lord: "As they called them [the prophets sent by God], so they [Israelites] went from them; they sacrificed to the Baals, and burned incense to carved images" (Hos. 11:2). The more God called, the more Israel rejected Him and rebelled against His love. Turning a deaf ear to God's prophets, the nation chose to practice idolatry instead.

God's Care

Like a loving father, God had cared tenderly for the nation during its journey through the wilderness after its slavery in Egypt:

> I taught Ephraim to walk, taking them by their arms; but they did not know that I healed them. I drew them with gentle cords, with bands of love, and I was to them as those who take the yoke from their neck. I stooped and fed them (vv. 3–4).

This statement of guiding and guarding Israel is tender and touching. The Lord took Israel by the arm to guide it over difficult obstacles so that it would not stumble and get hurt. When Israel fell during times of testing, God was there to heal its wounds.

God's love and compassion for Israel is like that of a herdsman who cares for his heifer. The herdsman repositions the yoke's strap under the ox's jaw, enabling the animal to eat its food with ease. With a handful of grain, the herdsman bends down and tenderly feeds his animal. God did not lead Israel as if it were a dumb animal, with ropes and halters. He guided Israel with cords of tenderness, kindness, and love. Compassionately and continually, he eased the nation's strain and burden. For 40 long years, God graciously provided food and water for Israel during its wilderness wanderings.

Israel was more than willing to enjoy God's generous gifts and gracious love. But like an ungrateful son, Israel took God for granted, disobeying His commands and disregarding His will.

God's Chastening

Although God is long-suffering, His patience has limits. As any good father should, He had to correct Israel for its ingratitude and rebellion: "He [Israel] shall not return to the land of Egypt; but the Assyrian shall be his king, because they refused to repent" (v. 5). Egypt symbolizes the new type of exile Israel would face in Assyria. With the collapse and capture of Israel's political leadership, the king of Assyria would control the nation's government. Thus Israel would have no king (cf. 10:3, 7, 15). Because the Israelites "refused to repent," their bondage in Assyria would be far more severe and last longer than their enslavement in Egypt.

Judgment hovered over Israel like the legendary sword of Damocles and, in God's time, would strike the nation:

> And the sword shall slash in his cities, and devour his districts [villages], and consume them [i.e., demolish the bars and bolts of their gates], because of their own counsels (11:6).

The sword would whirl around as it swept the land, devouring Israel's cities, villages, and defenses. Destruction would come on Israel because it prayed to Canaanite deities for deliverance from Assyria, rather than praying to the Lord.

Another reason for Israel's destruction was its continual backsliding: "My people are bent on [hung up on] backsliding from Me. Though they [God's prophets] call to the Most High, none at all exalt him" (v. 7). No one in Israel heeded the prophet's message because sin had lured the nation into a deep moral apathy.

God's Compassion

The Law of Moses required that every rebellious son who would not obey his father or heed his reprimand be put to death (Dt. 21:18–21). Israel was such a son. The nation flaunted God's love, took for granted God's mercy and compassion, ignored the many warnings of judgment, and deserved to be annihilated. But God's great love for His covenant people would not allow Him to abandon them.

God expresses His lament and deep love for Israel in four rhetorical questions:

[1] How can I give you up, Ephraim? [2] How can I hand you over [surrender], Israel? [3] How can I make you like Admah? [4] How can I set you like Zeboiim? My heart churns within Me; My sympathy is stirred (Hos. 11:8).

Admah and Zeboiim were cities that were annihilated with Sodom and Gomorrah when God rained fire and brimstone on them (Dt. 29:22–23). Though Israel deserved the judgment of Admah and Zeboiim, God's heart revolted within Him at such a thought. Instead, He turned from His fierce anger to show Israel mercy and compassion.

God has an eternal relationship with Israel. He chose Israel, called it, cared for it, and chastens it when necessary. And it is not His divine purpose to destroy it:

Thus says the LORD: "If heaven above can be measured, and the foundations of the earth searched out beneath, I will also cast off all the seed of Israel for all that they have done, says the LORD" (Jer. 31:37).

God will never annihilate Israel because of the promises He made in the Abrahamic Covenant. Although Israel will be severely punished for its sin, God always tempers His justice with divine compassion and will not obliterate the nation:

I will not execute the fierceness of My anger; I will not again destroy Ephraim. For I am God, and not man, the Holy One in your midst; and I will not come with terror (Hos. 11:9).

Nor will God return to destroy Israel as He did during the Assyrian invasion. On the contrary, He tempers His chastening with compassion and covenant love in hopes that His punishment will result in Israel's restoration and redemption.

Keep in mind that God's judgment on Israel, His son, is both punitive and remedial. Everything that befell Israel was intended to chasten the wayward nation back to God. No one can question God's actions: "For I am God, and not man, the Holy One in your midst [Israel]" (v. 9). God always does what is just and right, whether we understand it or not.

Abruptly, the subject switches to a future time when God will summon Israel back to the land for the Kingdom blessing of the Abrahamic Covenant. Hosea used a number of metaphors to express Israel's return: "They shall walk after the Lord. He will roar like a lion. When He roars, then His sons shall come trembling from the west" (v. 10). In the past, God destroyed Israel like a roaring lion (5:14). In the future, He will call Israel back to its land with His roar. During the return, "'They shall come trembling like a bird from Egypt, like a dove from the land of Assyria. And I will let them dwell in their houses,' says the Lord" (11:11).

No longer will Israel be like a "silly dove" (7:11), flittering around in confusion. It will be like a dove flying home, trembling with excitement as it returns in haste to its nest. In the future, the people of Israel will return swiftly to their land from all over the world to experience God's blessing in the Millennial Kingdom. This promise is affirmed by the words, *says the Lord.*

Chapter 11 ends with God representing Himself as a man enveloped by Israel's sin: "Ephraim has encircled Me with lies, and the house of Israel with deceit; but Judah still walks with God, even with the Holy One who is faithful" (11:12). Hosea had exposed Israel's unfaithfulness and hypocrisy through its lies and deceit. The nation had pretended to worship Jehovah while practicing idolatry. Although the King James and New King James Versions contrast Israel's faithlessness and insincerity with Judah's faithfulness, the Jewish Scriptures render verse 12 differently, showing Judah as defiant also. The Hebrew word *rud*, translated "ruleth" (KJV), means "to wander restlessly" or "to be unruly" against God. Judah, despite all its privileges (Temple, priesthood, covenant promises), was like a restless, unruly animal that cast off all restraints and wandered away from its master—just like Israel. Most commentators accept this interpretation, which seems to be the teaching of verse 12.

On the other hand, God faithfully keeps His covenant promises of redemption and restoration to "the saints" in both Israel and Judah. Likewise, God will bring redemption and restoration to a generation of Jewish people who will come to Him in repentance. In the Kingdom Age, Israel's sorrow will turn to joy as the once-wayward son experiences spiritual renewal through God's loving compassion.

CHAPTER 13

GOD'S DISCIPLINE OF ISRAEL

Two young boys were fighting in the park. A man took one of the boys aside and began to spank him for his inappropriate behavior. An observant bystander indignantly asked the man, "Why are you spanking one boy and not the other?"

The man replied, "The one I am spanking is my son, the other is not." As this story implies, wrong actions demand reprimands. Like the father who disciplined his son, so God chastened Israel.

Ignoring God's many warnings and past discipline, Israel continued to be a disobedient son. The nation indulged in deceit and lies and expressed its unfaithfulness to Jehovah through social injustice and reliance on political treaties with foreign nations. Such inappropriate behavior required God to discipline Israel further. But before doing so, He graciously extended one more opportunity for Israel to turn to Him in repentance.

In chapter 12, Hosea used Jacob to illustrate the type of commitment God desired from Israel. When God chastened Jacob for trickery and deceit, Jacob repented with renewed commitment to the Lord. God wanted Israel to do the same.

Israel's Diplomacy

Israel's unfaithfulness and deceptive foreign policies are depicted as wind: "Ephraim feeds on the wind, and pursues the east wind; he daily increases lies and desolation. And they make a covenant with the Assyrians, and oil is carried to Egypt" (Hos. 12:1). The east wind is called a sirocco. It is extremely hot and blows from the eastern desert, scorching man, animals, and vegetation. No rational person would want to be near such a storm. But Israel fed on the sirocco, grazing on such practices as idolatry, immorality, and social injustice—none of which nourished the nation but daily eroded its strength and eventually destroyed it.

Israel was on a dangerous and destructive course. Rather than trusting God for help, the northern kingdom of Israel made a political alliance with Assyria, then turned to Egypt for assistance in breaking it (2 Ki. 17:3–4). Israel's integrity was empty, like the wind, and brought the scorching blast of Assyria's anger on the nation. King Hoshea sent a gift of "oil" (olive oil) to Egypt in hope of securing the nation as an ally against Assyria (v. 4).

In Hosea 12:2, God widened the charge against Israel to include Judah: "The LORD also brings a charge against Judah, and will punish Jacob according to his ways; according to his deeds He will recompense him." The Lord presents Himself as both plaintiff and judge against all 12 tribes. The reference to Jacob includes the 10 tribes of Israel in the north and the two tribes of Judah in the south. God will chasten both kingdoms for their sin.

Israel's Discipline

Using illustrations from the life of the patriarch Jacob, the Lord tried to arouse Israel to forsake its sin. First, Jacob "took his brother by the heel in the womb, and in his strength he struggled with God" (Hos. 12:3). While still in the womb, Jacob's hand grasped the heel of his twin brother, Esau, (*Jacob* means "heel-gripper"). This action was prophetic, displaying Jacob's zeal and appreciation for spiritual matters. Years later, through trickery, Jacob gained the birthright and blessing of the firstborn from Esau, who afterward called him a supplanter (Gen. 27:36). Israel was supposed to exhibit a zeal for spiritual things, as did its forefather Jacob.

Second, on his return to Canaan after 20 years in Padan Aram, Jacob wrestled with an angel (the preincarnate Christ) at Peniel until the break of day: "In his strength he [Jacob] struggled with God. Yes, he struggled with the Angel and prevailed; he wept, and sought favor from Him" (Hos. 12:3–4). The Angel tried to make Jacob submit to God's will. When He could not prevail,

He touched the hollow of Jacob's thigh, putting it out of joint. However, Jacob would not release his grip until the Lord blessed him. Through this experience, Jacob learned to cling to God, not to his own cunning devices or to wisdom, experience, trickery, or strength.

Hosea also mentioned Jacob's experience with God at Bethel: "He found Him in Bethel, and there He spoke to us" (v. 4). This is the second time God revealed Himself to Jacob at Bethel. The first time was when Jacob fled home in fear of Esau (Gen. 28:10–22). At that appearance, God blessed Jacob with a new name and power, calling him Israel, which means "God strives," or "he who strives with God" (35:9–15; cf. 32:24–31). Thereafter, spiritual victories came to Israel through God's divine power and blessing, and God fought the nation's battles. The Lord also confirmed the promises He made to Jacob's grandfather, Abraham, and his father, Isaac. Years later these promises were confirmed to the sons of Jacob.

Hosea made it clear that the one who spoke to Jacob was none other than "the LORD God of hosts. The LORD is His memorable name" (Hos. 12:5). He is Jehovah, the covenant-keeping, unchangeable, self-existent one who commands the armies of heaven—both visible and invisible—and rules with unrestricted omnipotence on Earth, as in heaven. This is the name God gave Himself when He called Moses to serve Him (Ex. 3:13–15). God was able to deliver the Israelites of Hosea's day as He did their forefathers, if only they turned to Him in repentance.

Genuine repentance required the Israelites to change their conduct toward man and God. They needed to "observe mercy [meaning "love"] and justice" and "wait on [their] God continually" (Hos. 12:6), which meant allowing God to act in their behalf, rather than making decisions laced with deceit and lying schemes. What God required of Israel was obedience to the whole Law. He wanted the Israelites to show mercy and justice to others as dictated in the last five of the Ten Commandments. Such action would have displayed visible, sincere penitence. Israel needed to abandon its deceitfulness, as did Jacob, and come to God in repentance.

Israel's Deception

Instead, Israel embraced the practices of the Canaanites, its pagan neighbors:

A cunning Canaanite! Deceitful scales are in his hand; he loves to oppress. And Ephraim said, "Surely I have become rich, I have found wealth for myself; in all my labors they shall find in me no iniquity that is sin" (vv. 7–8).

The Canaanites originally were Phoenician traders whose reputation for fraud was well known. Israel, like the Canaanites, became wealthy by cheating people with dishonest scales—a practice prohibited by law (Dt. 25:13). The Israelites took great pride in their craftiness and boasted of their wealth. They were self-deceived and believed God would not hold them accountable; it was simply business as usual.

God was not ignorant of Israel's thievery and did not plan to allow the nation to go unpunished: "I am the LORD your God, ever since the land of Egypt; I will again make you dwell in tents, as in the days of the appointed feast" (Hos. 12:9). The Lord reminded Israel that He was its God since the day He delivered the nation from bondage in Egypt. And though He had delivered, protected, prospered, and settled the Israelites in a land they had not labored to acquire, He would nevertheless humble them by destroying their cities and driving them from their comfortable homes, luxurious dwellings, profitable businesses, and cultivated fields. They would become nomads. Furthermore, they would live in tents, as they did during their wilderness wanderings and the Feast of Tabernacles (Lev. 23:34–43).

God had warned Israel through prophets, visions, and parables (Hos. 12:10). Yet Israel turned a deaf ear to the messages.

Mockingly, God asked, "Though Gilead has idols—surely they are vanity—though they sacrifice bulls in Gilgal, indeed their altars shall be heaps in the furrows of the field" (v. 11). Gilead and Gilgal are mentioned to show how widespread Israel's iniquity had become, reinforcing the theme of the nation's deceitfulness in both religion and politics. Gilead was on the east side of the Jordan River, an area totally given to idolatry, sexual immorality, and wickedness of every sort. It was a rendezvous for bands of marauders who waited in ambush to rob, rape, and murder those who traveled through the mountainous area (cf. 6:8–9).

Gilgal was on the west side of the Jordan where Israel sacrificed bulls to calf worship and Baal. Here altars were as numerous and worthless as a heap of stones that a farmer stacks up at the side of his furrowed field. What took place in Gilead and Gilgal was indicative of the entire nation. There is a play on words here: Gilead and Gilgal would become *gallim*—Hebrew for "a heap of stones." God answered His own question: "Surely they are vanity [worthless]" (12:11).

Hosea returned to Jacob's humble beginning to remind the proud nation of how God cared for it:

> *Jacob fled to the country of Syria [Padan Aram]; Israel served for a spouse, and for a wife he tended sheep. By a prophet the* LORD *brought Israel out of Egypt, and by a prophet he was preserved* (vv. 12–13).

After Jacob fled to Paddan Aram, he tended Laban's flock for 14 years to compensate Laban for marrying his daughter Rachel (Gen. 29:20, 27). Like a shepherd, the Lord loved and cared for Israel.

Many years later, Jacob and his family went down to Egypt, where the Israelites grew into a multitude and became slaves to Pharaoh. God cared for them then, too. He raised up the prophet Moses to deliver them from slavery and cared for them as they wandered 40 years in the wilderness. The word *preserved* in Hosea 10:13 means to "keep sheep." Jacob kept sheep; and, in like manner, God kept Israel like a fold of sheep. As God had brought Jacob back from Padan Aram, so, too, He brought Israel back into the Promised Land.

The chapter closes with this statement: "Ephraim provoked Him to anger most bitterly; therefore his Lord will leave the guilt of his bloodshed upon him, and return his reproach upon him" (v. 14). Although God loved and cared for Israel, He was bitterly angered by the nation's gross immorality, idolatry, and indifference to His goodness. Israel required chastening for its sin. God did not remove the nation's guilt or penalty for shedding innocent blood, especially regarding its practice of sacrificing its children to the heathen god Molech (2 Ki. 17:17–18). This vile ritual insulted God, Israel's true Lord (Master), and intensified Israel's guilt and punishment. This explains the severity and length of Israel's chastisement, which has yet to come to an end. God's love for Israel has not changed. As He loved Jacob, so He will love Israel when its greatest hour of trial arrives in the future. Then Israel will embrace the Lord as Savior, and He will bestow Kingdom blessings on the nation.

CHAPTER 14

DEVASTATION OF A NATION

Although nations do not intentionally commit suicide, Israel was headed that way. Gross idolatry insulted the covenant relationship God had established with the Israelites, and their ingratitude toward Him for His grace and goodness had given them a spirit of pride and self-sufficient smugness. Thus Israel forgot the God who had lavished it with power and prosperity.

Hosea's warning of judgment fell on deaf ears. His preaching produced no change in the nation's commitment or conduct toward God. In chapter 13, Hosea reiterated and reinforced the message of the inevitable judgment that would result in ancient Israel's ruin.

Detestable Religion

After the split within the 12 tribes of Israel, Ephraim rose to superiority over the 10 tribes that became the northern kingdom: "When Ephraim spoke, [there was] trembling, he exalted himself in Israel; but when he offended through Baal worship, he died" (Hos. 13:1). The tribe of Ephraim had become great and was the leading tribe in the northern kingdom. The other nine tribes paid deference to Ephraim's authority and power. When one man in Ephraim spoke, fear and trembling seized the men of other tribes. But Ephraim instituted calf and Baal worship, sowing the seeds of death and sealing the nation's doom. It was only a matter of time before Israel's spiritual decay resulted in the nation's ruin.

God's warning had no effect on Israel. The Israelites continued to "sin more and more" and "made for themselves molded images, idols of their silver, according to their skill; all of it is the work of craftsmen" (v. 2). Idols filled their houses and groves. Instead of worshiping God, they worshiped molten images and prayed to deaf and dumb statues. They even paid homage and respect to the idols by kissing them—a sign of their total devotion to the pagan deity of Baal (v. 2).

The prophet used four similes to describe the nation's impending judgment:

Therefore they shall be [1] like the morning cloud [mist] and [2] like the early dew that passes away, [3] like chaff blown off from a threshing floor and [4] like smoke from a chimney (v. 3).

Israel would vanish as quickly as morning mist and early dew, which evaporate when the sun rises. Israel would be swept from its land suddenly and violently, like chaff on the threshing floor is scattered by a whirlwind or "like smoke from a chimney" is vaporized into nothingness. Hosea's stern warning should have provoked Israel to repent, but the nation remained untouched by the prophet's graphic illustrations.

Divine Rejection

The Lord reminded Israel of His unique relationship with the nation:

Yet I am the LORD your God ever since the land of Egypt, and you shall know no God but Me; for there is no savior besides Me (v. 4).

First, He told the Israelites that He and He alone had shown them grace and goodness from the time of their inception as a nation. He was the one who had delivered them from their oppressive slavery in Egypt. And He reminded them of the first commandment He gave them: "You shall know no God but Me" (v. 4; cf. Ex. 20:3). Israel had a special, exclusive, covenant relationship with the true and living God. No other deity had delivered the Israelites from their captivity in Egypt. Jehovah was their only Savior. Nor would any political alliance or powerful monarch be able to deliver them from their future troubles. Their worship of any other so-called god was meaningless and useless.

Second, He was their God in the wilderness: "I knew you in the wilderness, in the land of great drought" (Hos. 13:5). It was God who preserved them in the harsh wilderness by providing for their physical needs and protecting them from all who sought to destroy them.

Third, God prospered Israel in the land of Canaan: "When they had pasture, they were filled; they were filled and their heart was exalted; therefore they forgot Me" (v. 6). When Israel was "filled," it became satisfied, self-sufficient, and self-exalted, forgetting that God was its benefactor. Not only did Israel forget the Lord, but it also ceased to worship and serve Him (cf. Dt. 8). The metaphor in 13:6 speaks of a domestic animal that, in a luxuriant pasture, became headstrong and unmanageable. As did many before and after them, the people of Israel enjoyed the gifts but ignored the Giver.

Throughout Israel's history, God was like a tender, loving shepherd, protecting and providing for His people. However, that situation would change. Because they failed to accept His gentler means of correction, God's next method involved turning on them like a vicious animal and devouring them.

In Hosea 13:7–8, the Lord likens Himself to a number of wild beasts in His dealings with Israel. Like a fierce and hungry lion, God would rend the northern kingdom. With the swiftness of a leopard, He would lurk in hiding, watching for the appropriate time to spring on the defenseless nation and devour it. "Like a bear deprived of her cubs," He promised to "tear open their rib cage [heart]" (v. 8). When robbed of her cubs, a she-bear strikes at the perpetrator's breast with vengeance; and her claws tear open the person's chest, exposing his heart. Like a lion who slowly and methodically eats its prey in the safety of its den, God would consume Israel; and like "the wild beast [God] shall tear them" (v. 8). That is, as a pack of wild animals descends on its prey, God in His fury would descend on and devour Israel. Such a vivid picture is a fearful reminder of God's wrath, which will fall on all who reject His mercy and grace for a life of sin.

Declared Destruction

Israel orchestrated its own destruction: "O Israel, you are destroyed, but your help is from Me" (v. 9). A more literal translation of this verse is, "It has destroyed you, O Israel, that you have been against me, against your help." The kingdom's sin led to its demise. The nation trusted in idols and alliances with other countries, alienating itself from the Lord. The Israelites' prideful self-reliance severed them from God—the only one who truly could protect and deliver them from destruction.

Early in its history, Israel had exchanged God's gift of an infallible theocracy for a fallible monarchy (cf. 1 Sam. 8). With intonations of sarcastic scorn, God asked Israel two rhetorical questions concerning the rulers they had chosen to save them:

> I will be your King; where is any other, that he may save you in all your cities? And [where are] your judges to whom you said, "Give me a king and prince"? (Hos. 13:10).

The implied answer is that these elected leaders were nowhere to be found. Moreover, they were totally incapable of delivering Israel from Assyria's coming invasion. But the Lord, who alone is Israel's King forever, will be the nation's only hope for deliverance.

God honored Israel's request for a king after the 10 tribes split from Judah: "I gave you a king in My anger, and took him away in My wrath" (v. 11). Although God gave Israel a succession of kings, beginning with Jeroboam I (1 Ki. 12:20) and ending with Hoshea, He removed them all because of their extreme wickedness (2 Ki. 17:6).

God informed Israel that it would not escape judgment: "The iniquity of Ephraim is bound up; his sin is stored up" (Hos. 13:12). The document describing Israel's sin and sentence would be recorded, bound up, and stored in heaven—as a precious treasure is secured in a safe—until the day of God's judgment.

Time was running out. If Israel was to experience deliverance, it had to turn to the Lord immediately. Otherwise, the nation would become as a "woman in childbirth" and an "unwise son" (v. 13). Its suffering would be as inescapable and agonizing as the pain of childbirth. The baby, referring to Israel, is described figuratively as an "unwise son" who does not know enough to be born at the proper time. Such a delay results in the baby's death.

Hosea continued:

I will ransom them from the power of the grave [sheol]; I will re-
deem them from death. O Death, I will be your plagues! O Grave,
I will be your destruction! Pity is hidden from My eyes (v. 14).

Some believe this verse teaches that Israel is irreversibly
doomed. They support their position from the context of chapter
13 (vv. 7–13, 15–16) and interpret the first two clauses as interrogatives: "Will I . . . ransom them from the power of the grave
[sheol]? Will I redeem them from death?"—expecting a negative
answer.

Others interpret verse 14 as a promise of hope for Israel's
deliverance. The latter interpretation is supported by a long
history of Bible translations going back to the ancient Septua-
gint. Also, there is no indication from the text that the first two
phrases are interrogatives.

As for the objection that the promise of redemption is out of
context with the pronouncement of doom in this chapter, we
should keep in mind that God often interjects a word of hope in
judgment passages. The phrase *pity is hidden from My eyes* means
that God will not change His mind or His promise to redeem
Israel. The apostle Paul used this verse in 1 Corinthians 15:55–57
to declare the Christian's triumph over death through Christ's
death and resurrection. The ransom price for Israel's sin has
been paid through Christ. One day Israel will receive Jesus as its
Messiah and experience redemption and resurrection as a
nation.

The closing verses of this chapter present Hosea's final judgment speech. The prophet described judgment as "an east wind
[a sirocco]" from the Lord (Hos. 13:15). The wind is a picture
of the Assyrian invasion that completely and unexpectedly will
destroy Israel's kingdom like an east wind that dries up "spring"
and "fountain" (v. 15). Assyria will spoil the "treasury of every
desirable prize" by carrying off Israel's gold, silver, jewels, and
precious treasures (v. 15).

The prophet concluded chapter 13 with a specific word of
judgment against Samaria, the capital of the northern kingdom:

Samaria is held guilty, for she has rebelled against her God. They
shall fall by the sword, their infants shall be dashed in pieces, and
their women with child ripped open (v. 16).

Samaria was responsible for promoting Israel's rebellion against the Lord. It will suffer dearly for its sin. The city will be destroyed and its people slaughtered inhumanly. Babies will be smashed on the rocks without mercy and pregnant women ripped open to deprive Israel of a future generation.

Nations today should take note of Israel's sad experience and the high price it paid for forsaking God. When a nation smugly struts its self-sufficiency and forgets that it is God who provides its prosperity, peace, and power, that nation treads a path of spiritual and physical suicide. Pray that the nation you live in will heed this warning from God's eternal Word.

CHAPTER 15

ISRAEL'S FUTURE REDEMPTION

It is never easy for people to confess their mistakes. Whether it is a spouse seeking to rebuild a marriage or an individual seeking redemption from God, admitting blame usually is difficult. And it was difficult for ancient Israel. In the days of Hosea the prophet, the Lord sought to redeem His Chosen People from their lives of spiritual infidelity and immorality by convincing them to return to Him. In chapter 14, Hosea closed his revelation with a final plea regarding what Israel must do to receive forgiveness of sin and be reconciled to the Lord.

A Plea to Repent

Hosea clearly stated that before Israel can be restored, it must come to the Lord in repentance:

O Israel, return to the LORD your God, for you have stumbled because of your iniquity; take words with you, and return to the LORD. Say to Him, "Take away all iniquity; receive us graciously, for we will offer the sacrifices of our lips" (14:1–2).

The prophet's call for repentance is a major theme of this book (2:7–9; 3:5; 5:4; 7:10, 16; 11:5; 12:6), occurring four times in this chapter alone (vv. 1–2, 4, 7). Israel's return was not to be halfway or halfhearted but a total surrender to the Lord.

Hosea provided three conditions that Israel must meet before it can be reconciled to God. First, Israel's "words" of repentance must express a heartfelt prayer for pardon as it confesses its sins to the Lord (v. 2). Second, in turning to Him with its whole heart, not its lips alone, Israel must petition God to remove its specific sin of "iniquity" (v. 2). The word *iniquity* best describes Israel's rebellion, deceitfulness, and perversity. The Gentiles, of course, were also guilty (if not guiltier) of iniquity. However, other portions of Scripture discuss God's judgment of the Gentiles. The book of Hosea deals with God's people, Israel. Finally, Israel's people must ask the Lord to receive them "graciously" (v. 2).

The Lord will receive Israel when the nation comes to Him in a spirit of repentance, using the words He requires. In the past, Israel offered sacrifices out of habit. Now the nation must propitiate God, not by sacrifices or gifts of gold and silver, but by rendering Him the "sacrifice [fruit] of our lips" (v. 2). In other words, Israel was to worship God sincerely, by expressing heartfelt praise when seeking forgiveness, rather than by merely offering the perfunctory animal sacrifices.

Israel's words must be accompanied by actions. If the nation is to receive God's forgiveness, it must forsake three besetting sins: its trust in foreign alliances and military equipment, and its idols. The nation must renounce reliance on Assyria for help, deliverance, and security and depend instead on God. It must say, "We will not ride on horses" because horses and chariots were military equipment imported from Egypt for defense (v. 3). God strictly forbade the Israelites to "multiply horses," but they did so anyway in direct rebellion to His command (Dt. 17:16). This action showed a lack of trust in God. Israel was not to put confidence in worldly power or human aid but was to trust only in the power of the Lord for deliverance.

Israel also must stop practicing idolatry: "Nor we will say anymore to the work of our hands, 'You are our gods'" (Hos. 14:3). The practice of seeking spiritual help and blessing from deaf and dumb idols was to be forsaken forever.

In the final analysis, Israel must realize that its only hope is in God, where "the fatherless finds mercy" (v. 3). Man without God is like a fatherless creature that is no better off than a weak, forlorn orphan. Being an orphan implies a lack of identity, parental relationship, and care. Without God, Israel is fatherless, friendless, and helpless, like so many poor orphans.

Earlier in this book, Hosea named his children "not pitied" and "not my people," symbolizing that God had severed His relationship with Israel. Deprived of all help, Israel will come to realize that God alone provides mercy, love, forgiveness, and ultimate deliverance.

A Promise to Restore

God will respond to Israel with compassion and consolation when the nation comes to Him in genuine repentance, with a contrite heart. Then He will grant it favor and forgiveness, restoring it in three ways. First, He "will heal" its "backsliding [apostasy]" (v. 4). Such healing includes curing its idolatry, rebellion, and immorality and renewing its covenant relationship with the Lord.

Second, God promises, "I will love them freely, for My anger has turned away from him" (v. 4). Despite centuries of rebellion and idolatry, the Lord continues to love Israel freely. His love for it is voluntary, spontaneous, and a free gift that is totally unmerited (cf. Jer. 31:3). Just as all believers today are justified freely by faith through God's unmerited grace, so Israel will be justified at the Messiah's Second Coming. Only then will God's anger turn away completely from His people.

Third, God said, "I will be like the dew to Israel" (v. 5). He will renew Israel's blessing and pour it out like heavy evening dew. Heavy night dew refreshes and revives a sun-scorched land and provides the moisture necessary to bring about new life—an apt picture of the Lord's blessing on Israel after centuries of a dry and barren spiritual life. Israel will experience this prosperity and fruitfulness during the Millennial Kingdom.

When Israel at last experiences redemption and renewed fellowship with the Lord, "he shall grow [blossom] like the lily, and lengthen his roots like Lebanon" (v. 5). A lily is a delicate plant that grows rapidly and reproduces abundantly, and its long stem bears a beautiful flower that emits a pleasant fragrance. Although the lily is beautiful, its shallow root system means it also dries up quickly and dies. Thus Hosea compared Israel's root in the time of its redemption to the cedars in Lebanon. Their roots descend deep into the mountain soil and easily support massive growth and weight, enabling the trees to grow strong, tall, and stately, piercing the sky. Israel, which has been uprooted often throughout its history, will, in the day of its redemption, be rooted in its land forever. The nation will be as strong and stable as the cedars of Lebanon because it will be planted in the Lord.

Hosea also mentioned three more results of Israel's redemption: "His branches shall spread; his beauty shall be like an olive tree, and his fragrance like Lebanon" (v. 6). These branches represent Israel's expansion and numerical growth during the Millennium. In that day, Israel's beauty will be like the olive tree, whose green foliage and fruit production symbolize the nation's holiness and spiritual vitality. Israel's fragrance will be like cedars of Lebanon, which emit an aroma that delights all who experience it. In the Millennium, Israel will be acceptable to God; and its loveliness, pleasing to man.

In verse 7, the simile becomes a metaphor:

Those who dwell under his shadow shall return; they shall be revived like grain, and grow [blossom] like a vine. Their scent shall be like the wine of Lebanon.

Some teach that this metaphor refers to the Lord as a great tree and to Israel as dwelling under His shadow in the Millennium. Others believe the tree represents the nation of Israel, to which individual Jewish people will return at the inception of the Millennial Kingdom. The latter interpretation is consistent with the similes of the previous two verses, which compare Israel to the trees of Lebanon. The people who have been regathered and restored to the land will be revived physically and spiritually, like grain that springs up in abundance. In that day, Israel will "grow [blossom] like a vine," a sign of great prosperity (v. 7). The "scent" of Israel's restored reputation will be like the wine of Lebanon that surpasses all others in aroma, taste, and value.

Furthermore, Israel will abhor idolatry: "Ephraim shall say, 'What have I to do anymore with idols?'" (v. 8). The nation will surrender completely to God and never practice idolatry again.

The Lord will accept Israel's repentance: "I have heard him and observed him. I am like a green cypress tree; your fruit is found in Me" (v. 8). After Israel's repentance and redemption, the Lord will be like a green fir tree, providing the nation with shelter and security. The fir tree is an evergreen, symbolizing fruitfulness from the Lord, who will supply every spiritual and material blessing that Israel needs in the Millennial Kingdom. What a change from Israel's situation in Hosea's day!

Appeal to Return

Hosea concluded his prophecy with an appeal for Israel (and people everywhere) to heed God's counsel:

Who is wise? Let him understand these things. Who is prudent? Let him know them. For the ways of the LORD are right; the righteous walk in them, but transgressors stumble in them (v. 9).

A wise person (one who can discern spiritual, scriptural truth) and a prudent person (one who lives according to it) will learn three lessons from Hosea's prophecy. First, the "ways of the LORD are right." They are the right path for us to take because, when we follow His ways, God guides, governs, and guards us in the way we should live. Second, "the righteous walk in them," meaning righteous people will obey God and, in so doing, experience and enjoy the Lord's blessing. Third, "the transgressors stumble in them." People who refuse to follow God's ways are transgressors, as were the people mentioned in Hosea's prophecy. Sin causes transgressors to stumble and fall, relegating them to the same unfortunate fate prophesied in this book.

God calls on the readers of His prophecy to repent, return to Him, and experience the redemption available to them. The prophet summed it up well when he wrote, "O Israel, you are destroyed, but your help is from Me" (13:9).

Despite dire circumstances, Hosea stayed faithful to God's call on his life, living with an adulterous wife amid a rebellious people. God honored Hosea's faithfulness, for in time, Gomer was reunited and reconciled to her husband. Although the prophet did not live to see it, one day Israel will be reunited and reconciled to God in righteousness. The Lord greatly used Hosea as he boldly proclaimed what was right to his family and nation. May Hosea's example inspire each of us to be more diligent and faithful in our commitment to the Lord in these last days.

INTRODUCTION TO AMOS

Amos's name means "to bear" or "burden-bearer." Amos was reared in Tekoa, a small town in the hill country of Judah, six miles south of Bethlehem and 18 miles from the Dead Sea. He was a shepherd or possibly a sheep breeder and a gatherer of sycamore fruit. He was a rugged, out-of-doors type of man, quite different from the society of Israel to whom he ministered. He was not schooled as a prophet but called from secular employment to bring a divine message (Amos 7:14–15). Unlike Hosea, Amos presented a straightforward message of justice to the political and spiritual leaders of Israel.

Though Amos directed his prophecy to the northern kingdom of Israel, he also had a message for the southern kingdom of Judah and the surrounding nations.

In the eighth century, King Uzziah in Judah and King Jeroboam II in Israel expanded their borders, took control of the trade routes surrounding their countries, and became extremely prosperous. An upper class society emerged (3:11–13) that built expensive homes (3:15; 5:11; 6:4, 11), enjoyed a carnal lifestyle (6:1–4), and exploited the poor (2:6–7; 5:7, 10–13; 6:12; 8:4–6). Political corruption ruled the day as the leaders oppressed the people and committed violence and robbery (3:9–10). Religious fervor was high, but it lacked a true devotion to God. Merchants did observe the Sabbath, new moon, and feast days but were dishonest and resented closing their businesses for religious days (8:4–6).

Amos prophesied during the reigns of Uzziah (792–740 B.C.) and Jeroboam II (793–753 B.C.), two years before the great earthquake (1:1; cf. Zech. 14:5). Though it cannot be documented, Josephus placed the earthquake during the time when Uzziah sinned against God by offering incense in the Temple (2 Chr. 26:16–23), which would have been around 760 B.C.

The theme of the book of Amos is that God's judgment will come on Israel, Judah, and the nations if they refuse to turn from their sin. Amos 4:11–12 is a key passage. A key word in Amos is *transgression* (used 12 times), and a key phrase is *I will not turn away its punishment* (repeated eight times).

OUTLINE OF AMOS*

I. Prologue (1:1–2)
   A. Time of Prophecy (1:1)
   B. Theme of Prophecy (1:2)

II. People Judged (1:3—2:16)
   A. Sledges of Torture—Damascus (1:3–5)
   B. Slave Trafficking—Gaza (1:6–8)
   C. Severing Treaty—Tyre (1:9–10)
   D. Sword of Terror—Edom (1:11–12)
   E. Sadistic Triumph—Ammon (1:13–15)
   F. Spoiling Tombs—Moab (2:1–3)
   G. Spurning the Torah—Judah (2:4–5)
   H. Social Transgressions—Israel (2:6–16)

III. Purpose of the Judgment (3:1—6:14)
   A. Ruined Relationship—First Message (3:1–15)
      1. Privilege of Israel (3:1–2)
      2. Parabolic Illustrations (3:3–8)
      3. Publish the Invitation (3:9–10)
      4. People Invaded (3:11–15)
   B. Refusal to Repent—Second Message (4:1–13)
      1. Rich Corrupted (4:1–3)
      2. Religious Compromise (4:4–5)
      3. Resisting Chastening (4:6–11)
      4. Revealed Confrontation (4:12–13)
   C. Repentance Requested—Third Message (5:1–17)
      1. Prophet's Lament (5:1–3)
      2. Provision for Life (5:4–9)
      3. Perverting the Law (5:10–15)
      4. Punishment for Sin (5:16–17)
   D. Ritual Reviewed—Fourth Message (5:18–27)
   E. Rich at Rest—Fifth Message (6:1–14)
      1. Charge Declared (6:1–3)
      2. Comforts Described (6:4–6)
      3. Country Destroyed (6:7 11)
      4. Confidence Denounced (5:12–14)

IV. Pictures of Judgment (7:1—9:10)
  A. Judgment Diverted—Vision of Locusts (7:1–3)
  B. Judgment Delayed—Vision of Fire (7:4–6)
  C. Judgment Determined—Vision of Plumb Line (7:7–9)
  D. Judgmental Dialogue—Voice of the Priest (7:10–13)
  E. Judgment Described—Voice of the Prophet (7:14–17)
  F. Judgment Declared—Vision of Summer Fruit (8:1–14)
    1. Israel's Destiny (8:1–3)
    2. Israel's Deeds (8:4–6)
    3. Israel's Dark Days (8:7–10)
    4. Israel's Doom (8:11–14)
  G. Judgment Day—Vision of Lord on Altar (9:1–10)
    1. Revelation Provided to Israel (9:1–6)
    2. Retribution Poured on Israel (9:7–10)
V. Prosperity After Judgment (9:11–15)
  A. Possession of Israel (9:11–12)
  B. Productivity in Israel (9:13–14)
  C. Permanent Promise to Israel (9:15)

*Outline does not always follow chapter titles or outline in each chapter.

CHAPTER 16

GOD'S JUDGMENT: INEVITABLE, IRREVOCABLE

Buzz words concerning political and social justice often fill the air. The Russians in the past talked about *glasnost* (openness) and *perestroika* (reconstruction) in hopes of producing greater understanding and defusing tensions with the West.

Former U.S. President George Herbert Walker Bush, in his Inaugural Address on January 20, 1989, spoke of "a new breeze" blowing. "A world refreshed by freedom seems reborn," he said. "The day of the dictator is over." He also talked about making "kinder the face of the nation and gentler the face of the world."

At one time, the late terrorist Yasser Arafat talked about "Israel's right to exist," hoping to put worldwide pressure on Israel to give Arabs the "occupied" territories of Judea and Samaria and recognize a Palestinian state in the region.

While all this talk of political and social justice sounds good, not much justice actually exists. There is still political corruption in high places. The Russians and others still subjugate smaller nations. Third World countries are still exploited for political advantage, and the world still largely neglects and abuses the poor and needy.

Amos faced a similar world, as political leaders in the Middle East perpetrated extreme social and civil violence. To this world an outraged Amos was called from his secular work to announce a coming judgment.

Prophecy of Judgment

The name Amos comes from a root word that means "to bear" or "to place a load upon," aptly describing the type of message God had called this prophet to bring. The message of judgment came through a vision when Uzziah was king of Judah and Jeroboam II was king of Israel, "two years before the earthquake" (Amos 1:1). Using the prophecy of Zechariah 14:5, the ancient Jewish historian Flavius Josephus placed the earthquake in the time of Uzziah's transgression into the Temple.[1] Uzziah tried to usurp the position of priest and burn incense on the altar. So God struck him with leprosy for the remainder of his life (2 Chr. 26:16–23).

Amos portrayed the Lord as a roaring lion uttering judgment from the Temple, God's earthly dwelling in Zion and Jerusalem: "The LORD roars from Zion, and utters His voice from Jerusalem (Amos. 1:2; cf. Joel 3:16). This description was meant to chastise the northern kingdom of Israel, which had set up altars in Shechem, Dan, and Bethel—places where God had not put His name nor commanded worship.

A lion's roar, heard far and wide, strikes fear in the hearts of man and beast (3:8). Although he stalks his prey in silence, a lion roars when the prey is in his grip and a kill is certain.

The hot breath of God's roar would dry up the shepherds' pastures, impacting Judah and the lands to the south. His roar would thunder northward, sweeping into Samaria and withering the entire Carmel area, which usually does not experience such drought: "The pastures of the shepherds mourn, and the top of Carmel withers" (v. 2). This pronouncement should not have taken Israel by surprise because God had warned Israel that failure to keep its covenant commitment would produce the curse of drought (Dt. 28:20–24). Few of the Lord's judgments affect people as adversely as drought.

The judgment engulfed not only Israel but the surrounding nations. Scripture lists these judgments according to how severely a Gentile nation persecuted God's people rather than according to the nation's geographical location.

For a number of reasons, Amos began with the judgment of Israel's enemies. First, doing so would grab the Israelites' attention, and they would listen more closely. Second, it would show that God cared for them by judging their enemies. Third, the nation might repent, sensing that God was closing in on Israel for judgment. Fourth, Israel would know that God is slow to anger and patiently gives His people time to repent.

The denunciation of each nation begins with the same formula: "Thus says the LORD: For three transgressions . . . and for four, I will not turn away its punishment" (Amos 1:3, 6, 9, 11, 13; 2:1, 4, 6). Some interpret the statement to mean four transgressions added to three, totaling seven. Seven is a perfect number, thus indicating the cup of sin is completely full for God to bring judgment. It would be better to interpret this phrase as meaning that an incalculable number of sins have been committed, the cup of guilt is full, and God's judgment must fall.

Three principles about God's judgment need to be noted. First, the punishment is inevitable and irrevocable. Second, it is God who identifies the sins of a nation and announces the precise judgment. Third, God is long-suffering with nations, giving them time to repent.

Each nation's sin is described as a transgression, which carries the idea of breaking a covenant relationship through acts of rebellion. Israel and Judah had broken their covenant promise to God by disobeying the Law (Ex. 19:3–6). The Gentiles had broken God's Noahic Covenant by brutally shedding man's blood (Gen. 9:5–17). The nations had engaged in such barbaric and inhumane acts that God's judgment had to fall. God, in fact, holds all people responsible for their willful opposition to His standards (1 Pet. 4:5).

People Judged

Having set forth the purpose for his prophecy, Amos then announced the judgments on the nations. In each instance, he did not enumerate all the sins of a particular nation, but mentioned only the final sin (with the exception of Israel) that triggered God's wrath. The prophet approached each nation with the same pattern. First, he gave the reason God denounced it. Second, he presented its repulsive deeds. Third, he presented the results of its destruction.

SYRIA. The first nation denounced is Syria, identified by its major city, Damascus (Amos 1:3–5). Damascus would be judged for its ghastly threshing of Gilead "with implements of iron" (v. 3). True, God had allowed Syrian King Hazael and his son Ben-Hadad to smite the land east of the Jordan River (Gilead, Gad, Reuben, and Manasseh) for its sins; but the Syrians did so in a barbaric, brutal way (2 Ki. 10:32–33; 13:3–7). They ran over the captives of Gilead with a threshing machine consisting of long, sharp teeth on its underside, which shredded an individual's flesh.

King Hazael's repulsive action would result in the destruction of Damascus. Ben Hadad's palace (fortification) was to be burned to the ground: "But I will send a fire into the house of Hazael, which shall devour the palaces of Ben-Hadad" (Amos 1:4). Furthermore, "the gate bar of Damascus" would be destroyed (v. 5). And inhabitants "from the Valley [plain] of Aven" (most likely Baalbeck, a heathen worship center) and "Beth [house of] Eden" (plush summer palace of the king) would be cut off (v. 5). Those who survived would be taken captive "to Kir," the place of their origin in Mesopotamia (v. 5). This prophecy was fulfilled when the Assyrian Tiglath-Pileser destroyed Damascus in 732 B.C. (2 Ki. 16:7–9).

PHILISTIA. The second country denounced is Philistia (Amos 1:6–8), with its major cities: Gaza (capital), Ashdod, Ashkelon, and Ekron (vv. 7–8). Gath, the nation's fifth major city, is not mentioned. It is likely that Judah had already captured Gath before this prophecy was given, although Amos mentioned it as a city of Philistia (6:2; cf. 2 Chr. 26:6).

Gaza was a center for slave trading because of its location on the Mediterranean coast between Tyre and Egypt. Gaza would raid surrounding people weak in defense and deport the whole lot into slavery for financial gain. Those sold from Israel suffered great humiliation and abuse at the hands of Edom. The Edomites in turn sold their slaves to other countries for financial gain.

The Assyrian Tiglath-Pileser III attacked Gaza in 743 B.C., making a vassal city out of it and subjugating the entire area. Decades later the Babylonians under Nebuchadnezzar destroyed Philistia, its cities, kings, and people.

TYRE. The third nation denounced is Tyre (vv. 9–10), Phoenicia's major city. Tyre's transgression was that it "delivered up the whole captivity to Edom, and did not remember the covenant of brotherhood" (v. 9). Amos did not identify the captive people, but most likely they were Israelites bought by the Phoenicians and then sold to Edom for great gain.

The "covenant of brotherhood" could have been made between Kings Hiram and David (2 Sam. 5:11) or Kings Hiram and Solomon (1 Ki. 5:2–6; 9:11–14). This was a protective covenant between the participants. Tyre's action was totally unprovoked, for no Israelite king had come against the Phoenicians.

The result of Tyre's sin would be its destruction by fire. This prophecy was fulfilled when Alexander the Great destroyed Tyre in 332 B.C. after a seven-month siege. History records that 6,000 people were killed during the siege, and 30,000 were sold into slavery.

EDOM. The fourth nation denounced is Edom (Amos 1:11–12; Obad. 10). Edom showed no pity (compassion) on Israel and in anger tore it apart as a bloodthirsty wild beast kills its prey for sheer pleasure (Amos 1:11). Edom "kept his wrath forever," continually seeking opportunities to gratify its hatred for Israel.

Edom's transgression would result in its two major cities, Teman and Bozrah, being burned (v. 12). Thus the entire nation would be destroyed. The Assyrians subjugated Edom in the eighth century B.C. By the fifth century B.C., it had become a desolate wasteland and was later overtaken by the Nabateans, an Arabian tribe.

AMMON. The fifth nation denounced is Ammon, Lot's descendants through his younger daughter (vv. 13–15; cf. Gen. 19:38). The Ammonites had "ripped open the women with child" during their border raids into Gilead, trying to destroy Israel's population and grab Israel's land (v. 13).

Ammon's detestable sin would be punished by the burning of its capital city, Rabbah (present-day Amman, Jordan). The invaders would enter Rabbah shouting bloodcurdling cries of war and, like a whirlwind, destroy the city and its people (v. 14). This prophecy was fulfilled by Tiglath-Pileser III of Assyria when he destroyed Ammon in 734 B.C.

MOAB. The sixth nation denounced is Moab, Lot's descendants through his older daughter (2:1–3; cf. Gen. 19:37). Moab was located between Ammon and Edom, east of the Dead Sea.

The Moabites committed the despicable crime of digging up the bones of Edom's king and burning them into lime (v. 1). Although this incident is not recorded in the historical books, many scholars believe it took place when Edom confederated with King Jehoram (Israel) and King Jehoshaphat (Judah) to come against King Mesha of Moab (2 Ki. 3:4–9). Moab's sin would result in the burning of its major city, Kerioth (Amos 2:2; cf. Jer. 48:24, 41). The enemy would invade Moab with a bloodcurdling shout of war and the piercing sound of the trumpet (v. 2). In the conflict, its judges, princes, and people would be utterly consumed (v. 3). History confirms that Moab ceased to be a power in the Middle East.

JUDAH. The seventh nation denounced is Judah. Judah did not commit inhumane acts of savagery, as did the Gentile nations. But it "despised [rejected] the law of the LORD" and did not keep His commandments (v. 4). The Judeans lived as if the Law were irrelevant and practiced "lies which their fathers followed" (v. 4). The word *lies* implies deceit, but the Hebrew word can also refer to idolatry, as in this verse. Thus the prophet accused Judah of practicing idolatry like its forefathers.

God would judge Judah with fire that would "devour the palaces [fortification] of Jerusalem" (v. 5). This judgment took place in 586 B.C. when Nebuchadnezzar of Babylon destroyed Jerusalem and Solomon's Temple. He deported the surviving remnant to Babylon for 70 years of captivity (2 Ki. 25:1–21).

ISRAEL. The eighth nation denounced is Israel (Amos 2:6–16). Having gotten Israel's attention by pronouncing judgment on its neighbors, Amos now denounced the northern kingdom for its social sins. The prophet cited four major areas where Israel had not kept the law.

First is the area of *social justice*. The Israelites had perverted justice by selling "the righteous for silver, and the poor for a pair of sandals" (v. 6). For a bribe, judges condemned righteous people or possibly sold into slavery those who could not pay their debts. Such injustice was not legal in Israel (Lev. 25:39).

These cruel creditors "pant[ed] after the dust of the earth which is on the head of the poor" (Amos 2:7). That is, they oppressed the poor so severely the poor mourned by casting dust on their heads. Or they tread the poor into the dust of the earth.

Or the creditors took away even the dust that the poor cast on their heads in misery. In any case, Israel's heartless leaders did all in their power to destroy the meek (lowly and unassuming righteous people) by denying them due process. The creditors especially were involved (v. 7).

Second is the area of *sexual impurity:* "A man and his father go in to the same girl" (v. 7). This situation could refer to a temple prostitute or household concubine. The Mosaic Law sternly condemned such acts (Lev. 18:8, 15; 20:11). The men who perpetrated them "defile My holy name," said God (Amos 2:7). To disobey their covenant commitment in this area was tantamount to mocking and dishonoring God's name among the Gentiles (cf. Rom. 2:24).

Third is the area of *spiritual idolatry:* "They lie down by every altar on clothes taken in pledge, and drink the wine of the condemned in the house of their god" (v. 8). A person's outer garment could be held for a debt owed, but not overnight (Ex. 22:26–27; Dt. 24:10–13). A widow's garment, however, was not allowed to be held (Dt. 24:17). The Law commanded that such garments be returned by sunset to protect the Israelite from the cold. But the creditors kept the garments and laid them on the ground "by every altar" (idol temple) at Dan and Bethel to protect their own clothing, and they used the money they extorted to buy wine to worship "their god," meaning idols (Amos 2:8).

Fourth is the *sin of ingratitude.* God reminded Israel that He had delivered it from the Amorites, the most powerful enemy it had to face in conquering Canaan (v. 9; cf. Gen. 15:16; Dt. 1:20). The Lord destroyed this tall, strong people from their "fruit" to their "roots" (Amos 2:9). He reminded the Israelites that He alone delivered them from 400 years of captivity in Egypt and preserved them for 40 years in the wilderness (v. 10).

God had provided two groups of people for Israel's spiritual benefit: prophets, to present God's Word and will, and the Nazirite, to present a pattern for holy living (v. 11). But Israel rebelled against the prophets, commanding them, "Do not prophesy!" (v. 12). And they coerced the Nazirites to break their vows of abstaining from wine (Num. 6:3).

The Lord illustrated His judgment on Israel's ingratitude by saying, "I am weighed down by you, as a cart full of sheaves is weighed down," meaning He will press Israel with destruction just as a heavy truck presses the ground, leaving its tire print (Amos 2:13).

Israel's judgment would result in the destruction of the northern kingdom. Its defenders would not survive—not the swift, strong, or mighty (warrior) nor the archer, swift runner, or horseman (vv. 14–15). Even the bravest warrior would lose heart, strip off his equipment, and "flee naked" (v. 16).

The northern kingdom's demise was total and came at the hands of Assyria in 722 B.C. (2 Ki. 17:1–23).

This prophecy teaches a number of important lessons:

- God is extremely patient with nations, giving them time to repent before judgment falls.
- God is no respecter of nations; all will be judged for their sin.
- When the cup of sin within a nation is full, judgment is irrevocable.
- God is sovereign over all nations, choosing the time of their rise and fall.
- Nations are held accountable for brutal abuse shown to countries captured in war.
- God's standards for judging nations are similar, but the results differ.
- God brings judgment on leaders and nations that perpetrate fraud, oppression, and violence against its people.

Is the world headed toward social justice? Not according to the Bible! Paul said, "In the last days perilous times will come" (2 Tim. 3:1). Daniel detailed an upheaval among nations. Jesus said, "Nation will rise against nation" (Mt. 24:7). There is no new breeze blowing and no indication that freedom will be reborn. Nor is the day of the dictator over. Talk of political and social justice is just that—talk! Be vigilant! Arise like an Amos and give a message of warning.

CHAPTER 17

YOU ONLY HAVE I KNOWN

Israel had a special relationship with God. Like a father to his son, God heaped on Israel every provision for a life of purity and prosperity. Sadly, Israel turned out to be a prodigal son, rebelling against the goodness of his father by committing social injustice, sexual transgressions, and spiritual idolatry.

Like a father to his son, God punished this sordid behavior. Sternly, the prophet Amos thundered, "Hear this word that the LORD has spoken against you" (Amos 3:1). God had three messages for Israel, all beginning with "Hear this word" (3:1; 4:1; 5:1). And they were intended to be heard by the "whole family which I [God] brought up from the land of Egypt" (3:1).

Privilege of Israel

Israel was reminded of its unique privilege: "You only have I known of all the families of the earth" (v. 2). The Hebrew word *yada*, translated "known," means "to be acquainted with or to have intimate relation with." It speaks of God's covenant relationship with Israel whereby He elected it to a unique position among the nations and bestowed on it special privileges of love, care, and fellowship—something not granted to any other nation. God had chosen Israel to be His special people (treasured possession) above all people of the earth (Dt. 7:6–7; cf. Ex. 19:5; Dt. 14:2; 26:18; Ps. 135:4; Mal. 3:17).

Why did God choose Israel? It was not for its size, for it was the "least of all peoples" (Dt. 7:7). Nor was it for any innate goodness, for Israel corrupted itself immediately after its establishment as a nation at Mount Sinai following its deliverance from Egypt (Ex. 16:9; 17:3; 32:7–10; 33:3, 5). Scripture gives two reasons for God's election of Israel: His love for the people and His desire to keep the oath He swore to their fathers (Dt. 7:8). In that oath, God promised to forge the seed of Abraham, Isaac, and Jacob into a mighty nation and to give that nation the land of Canaan (Gen. 17:7–8; 26:3–5, 24; 28:13–15).

God chose Israel to be (1) the depository of His Word, (2) the nation through whom the Messiah would come (Gal. 4:4), and (3) a blessing to the Gentiles (Gen. 12:3). God's choice of Israel was pure grace; thus, it should not boast in its position or privileges.

One must ask the ultimate question: Why did God choose Israel and not another people? Only He knows! Paul put it best when he said that God chooses "according to the good pleasure of His will" (Eph. 1:5). The reason must be left with God.

With selective privileges comes sobering responsibility. In Deuteronomy 7:9–11, Moses enumerated seven principles about God's goodness that Israel was to remember continually.

1. "Know that the LORD your God, He is God" (v. 9).There is only one God. Israel should not seek help from or worship any other object or so-called deity.

2. He is "the faithful God" (v. 9). He can be trusted to keep His promises.

3. He "keeps covenant" with His people (v. 9). Israel is guaranteed that God will never violate or break the covenant He made with its forefathers.

4. He will show "mercy for a thousand generations with those who love Him and keep His commandments" (v. 9).

5. These promises were not made only with those who came out of Egypt but with their descendants as well, "for a thousand generations," or forever (v. 9).

6. Conversely, He "repays those who hate Him to their face" (v. 10). "To their face" means a nation will know personally that its judgment is from God.

7. And He "repays those who hate Him . . . to destroy them" (v. 10). The rebels will be destroyed. Thus every Israelite was to walk circumspectly before the Lord.

Israel is not the only people whom God has chosen. A great multitude of people from the nations of the world have been forged into "a chosen generation, a royal priesthood, a holy nation, His own special people"—the church (1 Pet. 2:9). God's divine purpose for both Israel and the church is that they show forth His praise throughout the world (Isa. 43:21; 1 Pet. 2:9).

With special privilege and responsibility comes accountability (Ex. 19:5). Therefore, God said to Israel, "I will punish you for all your iniquities" (Amos 3: 2). God's sentence of condemnation was great on Israel and Judah. They would receive "from the Lord's hand double for all her sins" (Isa. 40:2). The same is true for the Christian. His election does not negate His chastening if Christians live in sin. God will purge a believer's sin to make him or her a holy vessel for His use.

Parabolic Illustrations

Amos illustrated his point, that of accountability, with seven rhetorical questions. Through each one, Amos demonstrated that, where there is an effect, there is also a cause. Part B does not take place unless Part A precedes it.

First, "Can two walk together, unless they are agreed?" (Amos 3:3). The truth is self-evident: Two people cannot walk on a road together unless they agree to do so. Both God and Israel had agreed to walk with each other, but now the agreement was broken because Israel had walked in the opposite direction (Ex. 19:5, 8; 24:3, 7–8).

Many Christians break fellowship with the Lord and walk according to the ways of the world, "as the rest of the Gentiles walk, in the futility of their mind" (Eph. 2:2; 4:17). A believer, like Israel, is to "walk circumspectly" or diligently before God (Eph. 5:15).

Second, "Will a lion roar in the forest, when he has no prey?" (Amos 3:4). Lions do not roar unless their prey is so near it cannot escape. The roar will stop the prey in its tracks, while the lion moves in for the kill. God has roared out of Zion, warning of the judgment about to fall on His people (1:2).

The Lord expresses His displeasure to the sinning Christian, warning of coming chastening. Christians are to judge themselves, avoiding sinful thinking, habits, and actions (1 Cor. 11:31). Failure to do so invokes the chastening hand of God, not to destroy the believers but to correct their ways and conform them to the image of Christ (Rom. 8:29; 1 Cor. 11:32).

Third, "Will a young lion cry out of his den, if he has caught nothing?" (Amos 3:4). A young lion that has taken prey will let others know by growling. So it is with the Lord who had Israel in His grip and was ready to devour it.

Christians who live in continual disobedience are at the mercy of God, who can either temper His chastening or bring the individual to destruction. Chastening often takes the form of weakness; sickness; or, in some extreme cases, death (1 Cor. 11:30). The apostle John stated, "There is sin leading to death" (1 Jn. 5:16); it is the swift and immediate punishment of which Ananias and Sapphira are examples (Acts 5:1–10).

Fourth, "Will a bird fall into a snare on the earth, where there is no trap for it?" (Amos 3: 5). Naturally, birds can only be snared when they are drawn into a baited trap. Israel, which ignored God's warning, became trapped in sin that resulted in its destruction. The same is true for Christians who often ignore the traps set by Satan. Through lust, a Christian will take the bait of temptation and fall into sin, spiritually destroying himself or herself (Jas. 1:15–16).

Fifth, "Will a snare spring up from the earth, if it has caught nothing at all?" (Amos 3:5). Traps only spring when triggered by the captured prey. Israel, captured by the trap of sin, would not escape destruction. Likewise, Christians will eventually be caught if they continue to sin (Gal. 6:7–8).

Sixth, "If a trumpet is blown in the city, will not the people be afraid?" (Amos 3:6). A trumpet blast frightens people out of their security. Likewise, the prophet's voice frightened people when he spoke of coming judgment. Amos trumpeted the warning, but Israel did not hear or respond accordingly; thus, judgment was about to fall. When Christians do not heed the Holy Spirit's warning, chastening will come.

Seventh, "If there is calamity in a city, will not the LORD have done it?" (v. 6). The evil spoken of was not moral evil but physical calamity that God either allowed or sent as punishment to the city. The calamity Israel was about to suffer would be sent by God. Likewise, God often allows evil to come on Christians for disciplinary purposes (Heb. 12:6).

Amos applied the illustrations in two ways. (1) "Surely the Lord GOD does nothing, unless He reveals His secret to His servants the prophets" (Amos 3:7). God's judgment never comes arbitrarily. He revealed it to the prophets who, in turn, warned the people, giving them a chance to repent and reform. (2) "A lion has roared! Who will not fear? The Lord GOD has spoken! Who can but prophesy?" (v. 8). As fear naturally follows a lion's roar, so a prophet must speak God's message, no matter how distasteful or disturbing it may be. A prophet cannot be silent (2:12). As God's ambassador, he is under divine authority to deliver the message regardless of the opposition (7:14–15).

The first-century apostles also confronted opposition, boldly saying, "We cannot but speak the things which we have seen and heard" (Acts. 4:20); "We ought to obey God rather than men" (Acts 5:29). God is looking for such people today. Unfortunately, they are few, indeed.

Publish the Invitation

God had raised up Israel to be a witness of His holiness to the surrounding nations (Dt. 4:5–7; 28:9–10). But sin had extinguished Israel's light: "'See great tumults in her midst, and the oppressed within her. For they do not know to do right,' says the LORD, 'who store up violence and robbery in their palaces'" (Amos 3:9–10).

As a prosecuting attorney, God called Amos to invite the palaces of Ashdod and Egypt (Israel's enemies) to assemble on Samaria's mountains to witness His case against Israel (v. 9). They would witness "tumults," a state of confusion where justice and order had been overthrown. They would witness "the oppressed," those hurt by injustice and violence who were already graphically described (2:6–12).

Having rejected God's truth and light, the people lost all sense of justice. Their sin had so blinded and hardened them that they had no ability to discern right from wrong. So rulers stored up "violence and robbery in their palaces." They built massive palaces with plundered wealth, storing up the fruits of their wickedness, which was sure to bring judgment.

People Invaded

Israel was marked out for punishment. Its adversary would soon strike. The invasion was precipitated by King Hoshea, who refused to pay an annual tribute to Assyria. Shalmaneser V imprisoned Hoshea and besieged Israel's capital, Samaria, for three years. Sargon II came to power in Assyria in 721 B.C. and destroyed Israel's strongholds and palaces (3:11). And so the northern kingdom was destroyed in 722 B.C., and thousands of people were carried into captivity (2 Ki. 17:4–6). Israel's cities were repopulated with Gentiles who intermarried with the poorer Israelites remaining in the land (v. 24). These people became known as Samaritans, a mixed race of Jews and Gentiles, highly despised by the Jews (Jn. 4:9). This practice of mixing races was intended to weaken the population and prevent it from revolting against Assyrian occupation.

One often hears about the 10 "lost tribes" leaving Assyria and wandering through Eastern and Western Europe, eventually being discovered in Britain. Those who believe this teaching believe the northern 10 tribes to be today's Anglo-Saxons. This teaching further claims that Britain (supposedly Ephraim) and America (supposedly Manasseh) are to inherit the covenant promises God gave to Israel. This position, called British-Israelism, is fallacious and has promoted much anti-Semitism through various cults and churches worldwide.

The Assyrian captivity of the 10 tribes does not mean that Judah and Benjamin were the only tribes left. Before Israel's destruction, many within the 10 tribes went to Judah during the rebellion of Jeroboam (1 Ki. 12:16–20; 2 Chr. 11:16–17); thus Judah became the embodiment of the 12 tribes. Jesus came as the Messiah, not just to Judah, but to "the lost sheep of the house of Israel" (Mt. 10:5–6). The New Testament mentions people from many tribes (Mt. 4:13, 15; Lk. 2:36; Acts 4:36; 26:7; Phil. 3:5; Jas. 1:1).

Amos 3:12 explains that Israel would be consumed by the Assyrian beast as a lion rips apart its prey, leaving only small, worthless remnants. Those swept away by the Assyrians are pictured dwelling in Samaria on the corner of a bed and in Damascus on a couch (v. 12). The invaders would take all, even the inlaid ivory couches covered with expensive materials from Damascus. In the midst of their soft, sumptuous, secure life, the Israelites were quickly removed to servitude (6:4).

Israel's heathen enemies were not only to witness Israel's trial but to testify against Israel as well, the ultimate humiliation to God's people (vv. 9, 13). "The Lord God, the God of hosts" had the power and authority to execute the sentence of judgment (v. 13).

God's judgment would extend to the altars of Bethel, the seat of Israel's idolatry, where Jeroboam set up one of the two golden calves for Israel to worship (v. 14; cf. 1 Ki. 12:25-33). And the "horns of the altar shall be cut off," symbolizing the loss of any hope of refuge, protection, or salvation (Amos 3:14).

The rich and famous in Israel had winter and summer houses of ivory, built with extortion money from the poor (v. 15). These would be destroyed as well.

Many sense that America is wandering down the same path as ancient Israel did. The nation is full of social injustice, sexual immorality, and spiritual idolatry. The good life of peace and prosperity has lulled the nation into a false security. Preachers' warnings are not taken seriously; therefore, they go unheeded. Could it be that God's roar will soon be heard against this nation? Hear this word, O children of America!

CHAPTER 18

PREPARE TO MEET YOUR GOD

Israel had expanded its borders, taken control of major trade routes, and grown extremely prosperous during the reign of Jeroboam II (793–753 B.C.). An upper-class society had emerged and clothed itself in opulence at the expense of the poor. Political corruption ruled the day, as leaders committed violence and robbery against their people. Although calf and Baal worship saturated the land, Israel continued to worship God, keep its feast days, pay tithes, and offer sacrifices.

In the midst of this scandalous society, the prophet Amos spoke. His speech was not that of a sympathetic statesman, a placating prophet, or a tactful talker. He spoke with uncompromising boldness against Israel's narcissistic and national decadence.

Rich Corrupted

Amos began his second message with the declaration, "Hear this word, you cows of Bashan" (Amos 4:1). Bashan was located across the Jordan River, east of the Sea of Galilee. This lush, green area was ideal for grazing and producing fat, sleek, beautiful cattle (Dt. 32:14; Mic. 7:14).

The wealthy women of Israel were like beautiful cows who had grown fat and prosperous through a life of lazy luxury and self-indulgence. Amos pointedly accused these women of oppressing the poor (Amos 4:1). This they did by demanding more money and material goods from their husbands to satisfy their insatiable lust for luxury and drink (v. 1). Their husbands, in turn, squeezed the poor and powerless to acquire the finances needed to satisfy the demands of their wanton wives (2:6–7; 5:11–12; 8:4–6).

The character of these women reflected the society in which they lived: a soft, luxurious culture. Naturally, their children were being reared to perpetuate the same social, moral, and ethical values. These woman had so coerced their meek husbands that the men obediently pacified their wives' whimpering cries for more wealth. The women abetted in society's corruption by causing their husbands to compromise ethical business standards in order to meet their needs. They had no compassion for others; in fact, they crushed the needy (v. 1). They were the Jezebels of Israel.

God announced His coming judgment on these hard-hearted, corrupt women, indelibly imprinting two major points on them with a solemn oath: "The Lord [Adonai] GOD [Jehovah] has sworn by His holiness" (v. 2). (1) God is sovereign over all humanity, especially these women. They might have usurped authority over their husbands, who catered to all their whims; but God would not allow such behavior to continue. (2) He had "sworn," or vowed, on the basis of His holiness that these women would be brought to justice. A holy God cannot tolerate unrighteousness; He must act.

Their punishment would be awesome indeed. Not only would they be taken captive by Assyria, but they would not even be marched out the city gate with dignity. They would be driven or dragged out like cattle through the many huge holes within the city walls:

> "He will take you away with fishhooks, and your posterity with fishhooks. You will go out through broken walls, each one straight ahead of her, and you will be cast into Harmon," says the LORD (vv. 2–3).

One commentator stated, "Those who balked or refused to be led away would be forcibly snagged with large harpoons or fishhooks, much like fish pierced together and jerked over one's shoulder to be carried to market."[1]

The Assyrians led these women out of Israel and cast them into "Harmon" (v. 3) This is the only use of the word *Harmon* in Scripture, and scholars have been puzzled as to its exact meaning. Some believe it means "palace" or "citadel," referring to the palaces of Assyria where these women would be taken. Others believe it refers to Mount Hermon, which was the northern boundary of Bashan. Thus these women ("cows of Bashan") would be driven like cattle over the mountains (at the border of Bashan) on their way to Assyria. Either interpretation could be true within the context of this passage.

Religious Compromise

In a sarcastic tone, Amos called Israel to multiply its transgressions at Bethel and Gigal: "Come to Bethel and transgress, at Gilgal multiply transgression; bring your sacrifices every morning, your tithes every three days" (v. 4).

Bethel, you'll remember, is where Jeroboam set up a golden calf. Israel continually committed idolatry there (3:14). Gilgal is the first city where Israel camped after crossing the Jordan River, and 12 memorial stones were placed there to commemorate the event (Josh. 4:19–20; 5:9–10). It was here that Samuel judged Israel and worshiped (1 Sam. 7:16; Amos 5:5; Hos. 4:15; 9:15; 12:11). These were the two major worship centers in Israel.

Speaking with great irony, the prophet encouraged all Israel to commit transgression: "Come to Bethel and transgress, at Gilgal multiply transgression" (Amos 4:4). The word *transgression* is best understood as stepping over a designated boundary. Bible Scholar Gary G. Cohen put it this way:

> *The Hebrew word used here,* pasha', *primarily signifies "to break a covenant," and it is so used in 2 Kings 1:1. It is the fitting word, because those who came to participate in the false calf-idol worship in Bethel and Gilgal were "breaking God's covenant," namely the second commandment that forbade making or worshiping any idol (Ex. 20:4–5).[2]*

Although the Israelites continually practiced idolatry, they still maintained Levitical worship to the letter of the law. Amos sarcastically encouraged them to do so even more zealously: "Bring your sacrifices every morning, your tithes every three days" (Amos 4:4). The word *sacrifices* does not refer to an individual's offering but to the prescribed offering presented every morning and evening (Ex. 29:38–39). Amos also bid them to bring their tithes—not every year or, in the case of the second tithe, every three years (Lev. 27:30; Dt. 14:28; 26:12)—but, in ironic exaggeration, every three days.

He declared, "Offer a sacrifice of thanksgiving with leaven [literally, a burning praise offering], proclaim and announce the freewill offerings" (v. 5). They had broken the law of the thanksgiving offering in two ways: by putting leaven with the meal offering burned on the altar and by burning cakes with leaven reserved for the officiating priest (Lev. 2:11; 7:13–14). Sarcastically, Amos told them to announce the offerings of their gifts far and wide, "for this you love" to do (Amos 4:5). He was telling them their hearts were set on such actions because it satisfied their self-righteous spirits.

Here is the height of religious hypocrisy. God could never accept their gifts because the gifts had been acquired by oppressing the poor. No matter how zealous or accurate the Israelites were in keeping the Levitical law, worship from an idolatrous heart was an abomination to God. Their gifts were self-serving and self-glorifying, given only to impress others. God is not pleased with a multitude of gifts; He is pleased only with what is given with a proper motive from a clean heart. The Israelites were posing as people zealously committed to God while remaining idolaters.

Jesus criticized such religious hypocrisy. He condemned the Pharisees whose righteous acts and lengthy prayers were meant only to be seen by men (Mt. 6:1–8). By such behavior, Israel's religious leaders led the people astray. Jesus used strong language to describe such hypocritical religionists, calling them "hypocrites, "blind guides," "fools," "serpents," and "vipers" (Mt. 23:14, 16–17, 33). Christians must guard against committing similar acts.

Resisting Chastening

The Lord had chastened Israel hoping it would repent of its sin and return to righteousness. God had sent famine: "I gave you cleanness of teeth in all your cities. And lack of bread in all your places" (Amos 4:6). This famine is not recorded in Scripture. Notice how encompassing it was, affecting all of Israel's cities. But it still did not result in Israel's repentance: "'Yet you have not returned to Me,' says the LORD" (v. 6).

God had sent drought: "I also withheld rain from you, when there were still three months to the harvest" (v. 7). The prophet referred to the latter rain that came between February and April and was necessary if the crops were to ripen. God said one city received rain and another city did not, proving the drought was not random but was the sovereign act of God. It was so severe that "two or three cities wandered to another city" (v. 8) to obtain water. The word *wander* pictures the people staggering over a long distance to find a small amount of water that, when found, did not satisfy their needs. But the drought did not produce repentance: "'Yet you have not returned to Me,' says the LORD" (v. 8).

God destroyed their crops with blight (a scorching east wind), mildew, and locusts (i.e., palmer worms or caterpillars). These three plagues destroyed their gardens, vineyards, fig trees, and olive trees at the peak of their productivity (v. 9). Yet crop destruction did not produce repentance: "'Yet you have not returned to Me,' says the LORD" (v. 9).

God sent diseases and death, "a plague [sickness] after the manner of Egypt," referring to the many epidemics that periodically struck the nation. Likewise, Israel's young men were "killed with a sword" and their horses captured away. So great was the carnage that the stench of disease and dead, decaying bodies was unbearable to those still living. But the scourge of sickness and death still did not bring repentance: "'Yet you have not returned to Me,' says the LORD" (v. 10).

God destroyed some of the cities as He did Sodom and Gomorrah: "I overthrew some of you" (v. 11). The word *overthrew* describes a sudden and total destruction (cf. Gen. 19:25). Israel had been spared like "a firebrand plucked from the burning" (Amos 4:11), that is, like a burning stick snatched from the fire before being completely consumed. However, the near annihilation did not bring repentance: "'Yet you have not returned to Me,' says the LORD" (v. 11).

In Deuteronomy 28, God warned that failure to obey His voice and keep His commandments would result in famine; drought; blight; mildew; and eventual destruction by locust, pestilence, and military defeat (Dt. 28:21–24, 39–40, 42, 48–52, 57, 60). The entire land, he warned, would become like Sodom and

Gomorrah: "brimstone, salt, and burning," where nothing would grow (29:23).

Notice how God dealt with Israel. First, He exhaustively extended His unremitting love and long-suffering to this sinful nation. Second, He used different means to woo the nation to repentance: the respected Law of Moses, the direct word of the prophet Amos, and physical chastening. But Israel still did not heed God's warning. Even His rod of reproof did not produce remorse. In fact, the Israelites became more resolute in resisting His chastening. However, a people that continually rejects and rebels against God's loving reproof will suffer destruction.

Revealed Confrontation

The Lord was left with no alternative but to say, "Thus will I do to you, O Israel" (Amos. 4:12). What would God do? Amos did not say, thereby creating great apprehension for those marked for destruction.

Israel was told to brace itself for the terrors to come: "Prepare to meet your God, O Israel!" cried Amos (v. 12). Prepare, he was saying, to meet the God of wrath whose awesome judgment awaited this stiff-necked people. Yet Israel could have circumvented the calamity by preparing to meet God with a repentant heart.

Who is the God whom Israel will meet? What is He like?

OMNIPOTENT. He is omnipotent: He "forms mountains, and creates the wind" and "makes the morning darkness" (v. 13). The mountains are the most solid and everlasting manifestation of God's material creation, while the wind is an immaterial manifestation of His great creative power.[3] The phrase *and makes the morning darkness* is another description of God's mighty power to control creation.

OMNISCIENT. He is omniscient: He "declares to man what his thought is" (v. 13). God needed no one to tell Him of Israel's rebellion against Him or to reveal to Him the true nature of Israel's religious worship, for He knows what is in man's heart (Jer. 17:9–10).

OMNIPRESENT. He is omnipresent: He "treads the high places of the earth" (Amos 4:13). Here is a grand manifestation of God's might and majesty, showing His sovereignty over heaven and earth.

PREPARE TO MEET YOUR GOD

What is the name of this awesome God? He is called "Lord [*Jehovah*] God [*Elohim*] of hosts [*Sabaoth*]" (v. 13). Israel may ignore the prophet's warning of impending judgment, but it cannot ignore the One it will meet in judgment. He is Jehovah (YHWH), the self-existing God, the eternal "I AM" who made a redemptive covenant with Israel and delivered the nation from the mighty Egyptians. He is *Elohim,* the true and living God who has a uni-plural existence. He is *Sabaoth,* the powerful Warrior-God of Israel who encompasses every force or army in heaven and Earth. He is the One who marshaled all the armies of heaven to give Israel victory over its enemies.

But conversely, if Israel would not return to God in repentance, He would employ His armies against it. This pronouncement is tantamount to God declaring war against Israel.[4] And it would terrify God's people.

The following epitaph once caught the eye of a cemetery visitor: "Pause, my friend, as you walk by; as you are now, so once was I. As I am now, so you will be. Prepare, my friend, to follow me!" Under the inscription someone had scribbled, "To follow you is not my intent, until I know which way you went."

We chuckle at such verse because of its truth. Yet it is a sobering reality. We all must prepare to meet our God. The Scripture is clear: "It is appointed for men to die once, but after this the judgment" (Heb. 9:27). Those who have placed their faith in Christ alone as the final, sacrificial payment for their sins will meet Him in heaven with all its glory. Those who reject Christ will meet Him at the Great White Throne Judgment to be condemned to eternal damnation and the Lake of Fire, where they will pay for their sins themselves. Paul told the Corinthians, "Knowing, therefore, the terror of the Lord, we persuade men" (2 Cor. 5:11).

Are you prepared to meet God and to persuade others likewise?

CHAPTER 19

SEEK GOD AND LIVE

Israel looked like the picture of health. Religious zeal was at an all-time high. Israelites enjoyed unprecedented prosperity. Political order ruled the day. Peace graced the nation's borders. And Israel's prestige and power were at their zenith among neighboring nations.

But appearances can be deceiving. Israel was, in fact, chronically ill. Sin, like a cancer, had destroyed the nation's moral and social health, and death was imminent. For the third time, Amos sounded the warning: "Hear this word . . . O house of Israel" (Amos 5:1). It was God's message concerning Israel's sin and survival.

Prophet's Lament

Amos began this message with a lamentation (funeral dirge). Knowing the nation's destruction was near, the prophet mournfully sang of its impending and tragic death.

He pictured Israel as "the virgin," not implying that it was pure and faithful to God but that it had been protected from others; it had not been conquered or cast down. Yet it was described as "fallen" (mortally wounded), a country that would "rise no more" (dying). It was "forsaken on her land" (a corpse left to rot), with "no one to raise her up" (to restore it, v. 2). This is a ghastly prediction, to say the least.

Provision for Life

However, a glimmer of hope still existed for Israel. A long-suffering God with everlasting love for His people graciously extended a way out—the means by which judgment could be averted: "Seek Me and live," the Lord said (v. 4).

The word *seek* (Hebrew, *daras*) means to "search" or "seek with care and diligence," to inquire with the purpose of learning the direction for one's life. Life for Israel depended on the people seeking God in repentance and doing His will.

"But do not seek Bethel," Amos declared (v. 5). Such deliverance could not be found at Bethel, for it had become the center of calf worship, was now known as Beth Aven ("house of nothingness," i.e., wickness or idolatry), and was marked for destruction (vv. 4–5, cf. 3:14). Neither should they seek God at Gilgal, a place of idolatry that was destined for captivity (v. 5). Nor would Beersheba—where Abraham, Isaac, and Jacob worshiped—provide any hope (Gen. 21:31–33; 26: 23–24; 46:1). It, too, was corrupted with idolatry. No mention is made of Beersheba's fate because only the northern kingdom was marked for destruction.

Then the prophet made a more earnest plea: "Seek the LORD and live" (Amos 5:6). This time a warning was added: "Lest He break out like fire in the house of Joseph . . . with no one to quench it in Bethel" (v. 6). Failure to obey God meant He would bring inescapable destruction, like an unquenchable fire, on the 10 tribes.

Israel deserved such judgment. Its moral justice had turned to "wormwood" (bitterness) for the poor and innocent who could not afford to bribe dishonest officials. Thus national corruption "lay righteousness to rest in the earth" (v. 7), or cast it down to the earth, stamping it into the ground.

A third time the true, omnipotent God who rules over all called Israel to seek Him. Scripture describes Him as follows:

He made the Pleiades and Orion; He turns the shadow of death into morning and makes the day dark as night; He calls for the waters of the sea and pours them out on the face of the earth; the LORD is His name (v. 8).

Thus He is in control of heaven, having made the constellation of the seven stars (the Pleiades) and Orion. He is in control of life and death, turning "the shadow of death into morning" and making "the day dark as night." He can easily turn the threat of death into a bright morning of hope or turn a bright day of hope into a night of death and destruction.

He also controls nature: "He calls for the waters of the sea [evaporated into heaven] and pours them [rain] out on the face of the earth" (v. 8). He controls nations, raining "ruin upon the strong, so that fury comes upon the fortress" (v. 9). In other words, God, like a lightning flash, smites the strongest man or nation; and no fortress can stand against Him.

Who is such a God as this? "The LORD [Jehovah, or YHWH] is His name" (v. 8). The lifeless gods of Bethel, Gilgal, and Beer-sheba that Israel worshiped were nothing compared to Jehovah, their covenant-making and covenant-keeping God. The power of such a God should have convinced Israel to seek Him for their salvation and survival.

"Seek God and live" is a New Testament concept. In His dialogue with Nicodemus, Jesus used Israel's disobedience as an illustration of His provision for salvation (Jn. 3). (See Numbers 21:5–9.) Judgment came on the disobedient Israelites when God sent deadly serpents to kill them (Num. 21:6). Their only means of survival was to look on a bronze serpent that Moses lifted up on a pole (v. 9). Those who looked at it lived. In like manner, Jesus said He must be lifted up on the cross (Jn. 3:14; cf. Jn. 8:28; 12:32–34). And all those bitten by the "serpent" of sin and destined for eternal death could look in faith to Jesus and receive eternal life (Jn. 3:15).

Perverting the Law

Amos not only denounced Israel's corrupt religion but its cruel rulers as well. These rulers, he said, "hate the one who rebukes in the gate, and they abhor the one who speaks uprightly" (Amos 5:10). In biblical times, business and court were conducted at the city gate. The leaders hated anyone who upbraided the wicked rulers or spoke truthfully on matters of law.

Then Amos condemned those who oppressed the poor and took "grain taxes" from them (v. 11). Rulers bled the poor by charging exorbitant prices for handling the sale of their grain, and judges expected payoffs With the money they extorted they built "houses of hewn stone" (a sign of wealth) and "pleasant vineyards" (v. 11).

But God promised, "You shall not dwell" in those houses or "drink wine" from vineyards acquired by ill-gotten gain because He would soon destroy the nation (v. 11).

Through Amos, God continued: "For I know your manifold transgressions and your mighty sins: afflicting the just and taking bribes; diverting the poor from justice at the gate" (v. 12). Those who bribed the judges either never went to trial or received favorable verdicts. On the other hand, righteous people (those unwilling to pay) and poor people (those unable to pay) suffered injustices. The law strongly condemned such actions (Ex. 23:6–9; Dt. 16:18–20). God knew their sin and would punish them accordingly.

Since the land was full of corruption, "the prudent [kept] silent" (v. 13). A righteous man wisely holds his tongue in a totally corrupt society. Speaking out would not bring change; it would bring personal reproach and reprisal. Christ taught the same principle and practiced it before Herod and Pilate at His trial (Mt. 7:6; Lk. 23:9; Jn. 19:9–10).

Although the people wisely held their tongues, the prophet had to speak the divine message that God had called him to deliver. Again Amos thundered God's Word: "Seek good and not evil, that you may live" (Amos 5:14). In so doing, said the prophet, "the LORD God of hosts will be with you, as you have spoken" (v. 14). The Israelites erroneously believed that God's blessing was on them since they were experiencing great prosperity and were His covenant people. Actually, the opposite was true. If they refused to turn from evil, judgment was inevitable.

Americans often assume the United States is experiencing divine blessing because the country enjoys great prosperity. Such may not be the case. And even if it is the case, the blessing will not continue, given the moral decay and social injustice evident throughout the nation.

Although judgment had already been announced (2:6; 5:3), it could have been averted. Amos told the nation, "Hate evil, and love good; establish justice in the gate" (5:15). The people had to evidence a change of heart and begin to practice righteousness. If they did so, Amos told them, "It may be that the LORD God of hosts will be gracious to the remnant of Joseph" (v. 15).

That is, perhaps, in the midst of judgment, He would still spare a remnant and still show grace to those who hated evil and did justly.

Punishment for Sin

Amos predicted the sorrows that awaited Israel. He issued a solemn declaration, fortified by the weighty names of God: "the LORD [Jehovah] God of hosts [God of armies], the Lord [*Adonai*]" (v. 16). God, the sovereign Ruler of the universe, would personally lead His armies against Israel in judgment. The death wail would be heard in every street and highway by farmers, professional mourners, and those who worked in the vineyards (vv. 16–17).

Israel would be treated as Egypt had been treated during Israel's great deliverance from slavery there. God would "pass through" the land, touching every family with death and destruction (v. 17).

Amos cried, "Woe to you who desire the day of the LORD!" (v. 18). The Israelites believed the Day of the Lord would bring destruction to their enemies and blessing to them. But the opposite was true: "It will be darkness, and not light," "very dark, with no brightness in it" (vv. 18, 20). There would be no escape from the utter terror and death they would experience on that day. Although they might escape death from a lion or bear, they could be leaning against a wall in the safety of their homes and be killed by a serpent (v. 19).

Amos condemned their superficial worship in the day of judgment. Worship would not curry favor with God or avert the coming destruction, for it was mere formalism without faith or good works. God said He hated their empty worship; took no delight in it; and would not accept, regard, or hear it. He rejected their feast days, sacred assemblies, burnt offerings, grain offerings, peace offerings, songs, and stringed instruments (vv. 21–23).

God would respond only to justice and righteousness from the nation: "But let justice run down like water, and righteousness like a mighty stream" (v. 24). In other words, political, social, and religious justice was to permeate the land continually like an ever-flowing, mighty river if Israel were to survive God's day of wrath. This meant a radical inner conversion and outward commitment to righteousness.

Superficial worship was not new in Israel; it had existed from the nation's inception. God asked, "Did you offer Me sacrifices and offerings in the wilderness forty years, O house of Israel?" (v. 25). In other words, "Did you offer me pure sacrifices and offerings in the wilderness?" The answer, although not stated, was no. Israel's idolatry extended back to the days of Moses (Ex. 32:1–6). Stephen quoted this passage (Amos 5:25–27) as proof of the nation's idolatry as it wandered in the wilderness of Sinai (Acts 7:39–43).

Amos condemned Israel's worship: "You also carried Sikkuth your king and Chiun, your idols, the star of your gods, which you made for yourselves" (v. 26). Sikkuth was the Assyrian god of war sometimes known as Adar-melek, identified with the planet Saturn (called Kaiwan). The phrase *Chiun, your idols* may be a Hebraism for "image," or it may refer to many images made to represent Chiun. Wrote Merrill F. Unger: "The 'star of your god' probably refers to the representation of the planet Saturn on the head of the image of the idol."[1] Some interpret the word *Chiun* to mean the pedestal. Therefore, the idea, said Unger, is this: "You have lifted up the shrine of your king, the pedestal of your idols, the star of your god—which you made for yourselves."[2]

Israel had a choice: life or death. Its failure to seek the Lord in repentance resulted in its destruction as a nation and "captivity beyond Damascus," which history has documented to be Assyria (v. 27). Bible commentator Donald R. Sunukjian put it well: "The horror of 'exile' was more than the ruin of defeat and the shame of capture. For Israel, it meant being removed from the land of promise, the land of God's presence. Exile, in effect, was excommunication."[3]

America, like Israel of old, is no longer built on scriptural truth. We have experienced a fatal lapse of memory, forgetting the God who raised the nation to a position of power, prosperity, and peace, protecting and preserving its freedoms. The god of secular humanism has infiltrated all our institutions, making man the object of worship and God the object of ridicule and scorn. Morality has been replaced with immorality, where individuals are free to live an "alternative lifestyle" filled with the perversions that once made America blush. "Idols" of materialism cover the land, and the nation wallows in opulence and self-gratification. Like the once-great ship *Titanic*, America is headed for a fatal collision.

"The only thing men learn from history," it has been said, "is that men never learn from history." Although this is an overstated generalization, it is one we should heed nonetheless. Will our nation learn the lesson from prophetic history? Time will tell. In the meantime, we must call the nation back to God, for our survival hinges on seeking God to live.

CHAPTER 20

A WORD TO THE WEALTHY

The great 18th-century preacher John Wesley made a sensible statement concerning the use of wealth: "Make all you can, save all you can, give all you can!" Wesley was calling Christians to a scriptural balance in the use of finances. Although most Christians would give a hearty amen to Wesley's words, they generally live by a different creed: Make all you can, save some as you can, spend all you can on the good life.

The Protestant work ethic has brought the so-called good life to many American Christians, as they experience unprecedented prosperity in the 21st century. But with prosperity have come materialism, self-indulgence, and ease. Well-intentioned Christians often desire to obey Scripture regarding finances, but many have succumbed to a materialistic lifestyle.

Materialism and self-indulgence are not unusual problems when people become prosperous. Ancient Israel was no exception. In such a setting, the prophet presented his fifth message to Israel.

Charge Declared

Under Jeroboam II, Israel had expanded its borders, taken control of the trade routes, and grown prosperous indeed. Israel's neighbors viewed it as chief among the nations (Amos 6:1). A sense of false security had developed in Israel's leaders, and they began to "trust in Mount Samaria"; that is, they saw themselves as invincible and immune to destruction.

Amos opened his message with a strong indictment against these godless leaders who lived at ease:

Woe to you who are at ease [at rest] in Zion, and trust in Mount Samaria, notable persons in the chief nation, to whom the house of Israel comes! (v. 1).

They spent their days enjoying a life of extravagance, self-indulgence, careless revelry, and ease using money extorted from Israel's poor and wealth gained through the exploitation of surrounding nations.

Taking a page from history, Amos reminded the nation of what had happened to three great, neighboring cities that had followed the same godless lifestyle as Israel. They were destroyed. The first was Calneh (Calno, Isa. 10:9), an ancient Babylonian city built by Nimrod on the east branch of the Tigris River (Gen. 10:10; Amos 6:2). The second was Hamath, a major city on the Orontes River in northern Syria. It was later named Epiphania after Antiochus Epiphanes. The city was destroyed and incorporated into the Assyrian Empire. The third was "Gath of the Philistines," one of the five major cities in Philistia, south of Israel (Josh. 13:3; Jud. 3:3). It was destroyed by King Uzziah of Judah (2 Chr. 26:6).

Amos reinforced the lesson with two rhetorical questions: (1) "Are you better than these kingdoms?" (Amos 6:2). In other words, had these nations received greater prosperity from God's hand than Judah and Israel? The obvious answer is no. (2) "Is their territory greater than your territory?" (v. 2). Again the answer is no. He was saying, "Therefore, Israel, take a good long look at your neighbors. See how blessed you are compared to them. If God destroyed them, who had lesser blessings, how much more will He destroy you?"

But Israel turned a deaf ear to such a thought, putting "far off the day of doom" (v. 3). But how could the Israelites distance themselves from it when they caused "the seat of violence to come near" (v. 3)? They were actually enthroning violence and oppression through their wicked deeds. Israel's leaders were deluding themselves. In fact, their deeds were hastening the day when God's judgment would fall on them.

Violence was exalted shortly before Israel's destruction. Dr. Sunukjian wrote: "In the 31 years after Jeroboam II, Israel had six kings, three of whom seized power by political coup and assassination. The fear and violence in this period is reflected in the atrocities of 2 Kings 15:16."[1]

Is there not a parallel to the United States? No nation on Earth has experienced more wealth and prosperity than America. Few nations have been granted larger borders. No nation enjoys such a high standard of living and more time for leisure than the United States. But like ancient Israel, many gross injustices are being exalted, hastening the day of God's judgment. And also like ancient Israel, the nation seems to be turning a deaf ear to the preacher's cry that judgment is coming.

Comforts Described

Israel's wealthy leaders decorated their homes with opulent furnishings. Archaeologists have discovered that the Samaritans paneled their homes with ivory, squandering their money on such luxuries as "beds of ivory" on which they reclined in hedonistic revelry, arms and legs dangling over the sides in a drunken stupor (Amos 6:4, 6). They drank wine out of large bowls, most likely used in their temple worship for carrying the sacrificial blood (v. 6). This practice was the height of irreverence, to say the least. Notice that instead of sipping wine, they gulped it down from these holy vessels to satisfy their insatiable appetites.

They feasted on the choicest "lambs from the flock and calves from the midst of the stall" (Amos 6:4). These were specially fattened animals carefully tended and prepared only for the wealthy.

In their drunken stupors they frolicked in song, chattering childishly "to the sound of stringed instruments" (v. 5). Like King David, they "invent[ed] for [themselves] musical instruments" (v. 5). David used these instruments for God's glory, but these corrupt leaders used them for godless gaiety (1 Chr. 15:16; 23:5; 2 Chr. 29:26–27). No expense was spared to acquire fragrant ointments (oils) to pamper their flesh (Amos 6:6).

Living in such luxury had made these leaders insensitive and indifferent to the crisis facing the nation. They did not grieve "for the affliction of Joseph" (v. 6). That is, the flood of corruption did not distress them and move them to correct the situation.

Many Christians in the West are truly "at ease in Zion." Though their homes may not be decorated with ivory, they are often overflowing with luxury and the latest decor. Family rooms are often equipped with high-tech, state-of-the-art audiovisual equipment that caters to an ever-increasing appetite for ease and entertainment.

Although lamb may not be the gourmet food of choice for most Christians, many spare no expense to be well fed. Though they may not indulge in drink and song, far too often they spend every spare moment on personal pleasure. Though many might never think of getting rich by oppressing the poor, they sometimes yield to pressure and compromise their conduct in the business world. Selfishness and unethical practices are often stepping stones in the struggle for survival or secular success.

Unfortunately, too many Western believers waste precious resources pampering themselves with the latest fragrances and fashions while doing little to help their brethren being persecuted in other parts of the world. Egoism has made many believers insensitive and indifferent to the afflictions of other Christians. In the place of true compassion and involvement, many give only token aid to the needy in order to pacify their guilty consciences.

Country Destroyed

God turned out the lights in ancient Israel. The party was over for those reclining on beds of ease. They would be the first taken into captivity. Israel's leaders had wanted preeminence in wealth and wanton living; therefore, they would have preeminence in exile (v. 7).

The coming judgment was immutable and inevitable: "The Lord GOD has sworn by Himself," said the prophet. He had made an oath with Himself, solemnized by His holy name, that He, "the LORD God of hosts [battle]," would make war against Israel for the following reason: "I abhor [loathe] the pride [of exaltation] of Jacob, and hate his palaces [citadels]" (v. 8). In Hebrew the thought is more pungent: I loathe the pride of Jacob's exaltation, and his citadels I hate! The Hebrew text begins and ends with the word *hate*. God hated Israel's palaces, built and filled with wealth extorted from the poor (cf. 3:10). Thus He had no choice but to consign Israel to destruction and captivity (v. 8).

Amos predicted the terror to come on Israel, when the nation would be turned over to its enemy. Even if some—a remnant—escape from the sword ("ten men remain in one house," v. 9), they will still die, possibly from the effects of famine or disease.

With so many family members slain during the siege, other relatives, such as "a relative of the dead," will be called on to dispose of the bodies (v. 10). They will have to be burned rather than buried, for one of two reasons: Either there will be too many to dispose of or the siege around the city will make burial outside Samaria's walls impossible. It was Israel's custom to burn rather than bury the body of an extremely wicked individual (Lev. 20:14; 21:9). This pronouncement was a bitter testimony against Samaria's wickedness.

The Israelites also will be forbidden to "mention the name of the LORD" (Amos 6:10). Perhaps it would be inappropriate for them to mention God's name since He will have brought the destruction on them. Perhaps they will be forbidden to mention it because they were so sinful. Or perhaps the religious leaders will forbid the mention of God's name because the people will blame Him for their destruction, and they will fear that mentioning His name will cause the Lord to send even more judgment on the survivors. Whatever the reason, God's name will not be heard during this disaster.

Amos also prophesied that none would escape the invasion: "He will break the great house into bits, and the little house into pieces" (v. 11). The rich man's home will be leveled to the ground, and the poor man's will be torn apart. God is no respecter of persons. When His judgment falls, rich and poor alike will be destroyed. Just as in war, young and old and rich and poor all suffer.

Confidence Denounced

Israel was living with a false sense of security. Material prosperity and military protection had lulled the nation into believing it was immune to destruction. With two questions, Amos proved such confidence was ludicrous: "Do horses run on rocks? Does one plow there with oxen?" (v. 12). Certainly not. Such action was useless, foolish, and contrary to nature. In like manner, it was ridiculous for Israel to believe that its military power was capable of destroying its enemies because God would not spare a people who had "turned justice into gall [poison], and the fruit of righteousness into wormwood" (v. 12). Deliverance will be nonexistent. Israel had poisoned the very judicial system established to preserve the nation, the fruit of which will be bitter destruction.

Israel had boasted, "Have we not taken Karnaim [KJV: horns] for ourselves by our own strength?" (v. 13). Horns symbolize an animal's glory and power. Recent military victories under Jeroboam II had given Israel a false sense of prowess and power so that the nation felt invincible to surrounding enemies (2 Ki. 14:25–27). But God had the last word concerning Israel's security. To rejoice over its own power was like rejoicing "over Lo Debar [nothing]" (Amos 6:13). God will soon raise up a nation to afflict Israel "from the entrance of Hamath to the Valley of the Arabah" (v. 14). Israel's destruction will extend from the Sea of Galilee to the Gulf of Aqaba. And the nation will be afflicted by its enemy; that is, taken out of Samaria into slavery (v. 14).

America's Founding Fathers realized that, like Israel, this nation was not born by accident but by divine design. Like Israel, America's security and survival do not rest in its political savvy, powerful military, or prosperous economy but in the righteousness of its people. To retain its freedom and greatness, America needs to avoid duplicating Israel's sins, so graphically described here, or it will become smug and secure in its superpower status and suffer the consequences.

Today the United States is steering toward troubled waters. The masses have forgotten—or worse, are overtly rejecting—God. Our only defense rests in the conviction, character, and commitment of Christians who love the Lord and want to serve Him. But if Christians are "at ease in Zion," totally immersed in egoism, how much longer will the nation survive?

Will the nation continue wallowing in materialism, self-indulgence, ease, and entertainment with little concern for God's priorities in our lives? Or will we set new spiritual priorities? Isn't it time to have a word with yourself about wealth?

CHAPTER 21

THE FATAL VISION

In the 21st century, futurists are busy forecasting sweeping global changes precipitated by dramatic advances in technology. They hope such changes will bring worldwide peace and prosperity. Other prognosticators view such talk as a ploy to bring material prosperity to third-world countries in hopes that it will precipitate worldwide peace. In reality, however, the world is like a time bomb ready to explode, with little hope for global peace in the near future.

When it comes to predicting the future, psychics and astrologers have always had faulty vision. For example, in 1986 author Ralph Blodgett wrote the following: "Of 550 specific predictions made by the nation's leading psychics and astrologers at the beginning of 1985, only 24 of them (less than 5 percent) actually happened as the psychics said they would, and 526 (more than 95 percent) failed to come to pass."[1]

Furthermore, all of these psychics and astrologers missed the 25 critical news events of 1985. One thing is sure: they could not predict the future. In fact, God condemns such people (Dt. 13:1–11; 18:9–14).

Yet, a small group of Israelite prophets, called by God, accurately foretold a number of future events. For example, the prophet Amos was given a vision concerning Israel's future ruin. In the final section of his book, Amos recorded five such visions, four of which began with the words, *Thus the Lord GOD showed me* (Amos 7:1, 4, 7; 8:1). Three of the five fatal visions are recorded in chapter 7.

The Vision of Plague

God showed Amos a great swarm of locusts, which He was preparing to unleash on Israel. Amos prophesied that the plague would come "at the beginning of the late crop; . . . after the king's mowings" (Amos 7:1). It was customary for the king to tax the people by taking the first cutting of the hay crop to feed his own livestock. The people kept the late crop as fodder for their own animals.

Amos pictured the plague as taking place after the farmer's winter crop was depleted, when he needed the final growth to feed his livestock. When the locusts would finish eating "the grass of the land," no vegetation would remain for either man or animal (v. 2). Although this vision refers to a literal plague of locusts descending on Israel, it also symbolizes the great destruction that will come at the hands of the Assyrians.

Amos pled with the Lord to spare the nation: "O Lord GOD, forgive, I pray! Oh, that Jacob may stand, for he is small!" (v. 2). The prophet's petition was not based on Israel's goodness, because the nation was guilty and deserved judgment. Rather, he appealed to God's grace for survival.

God responded with a promise: "So the LORD relented [repented] concerning this. 'It shall not be,' said the LORD" (v. 3). What does it mean that God "repented"? How can a perfect God repent? Does God change His mind? A distinction must be made between God's character and His action toward man. God's attributes work together in perfect harmony; they cannot contradict one another. It cannot be said that God changes His purpose or mind when it comes to bringing judgment on sin. But God will change His action (i.e., withhold judgment) when a person or nation truly repents. Therefore, repentance on God's part involves a proper, divine reaction to man's sin; that is, God will either extend mercy or judgment. God honored Amos's intercessory prayer by showing mercy to Israel. He withheld His hand of judgment, thus giving the nation more time to repent of its sin.

A number of principles concerning God's judgment can be drawn from this text. First, God does hear those who intercede for a nation; thus He may act on the prayers of His people on that nation's behalf. Second, the Lord longs to extend grace, not judgment, to people who forsake sin. Third, even though judgment on a nation may be imminent, God will often divert His judgment and give a nation more time to repent.

The Vision of Fire

In the second vision, Amos was shown a plague of fire that threatened to destroy the entire land. The Lord "called for conflict by fire"; that is, He summoned the fire to judge Israel (v. 4). The fire would consume "the great deep," or dry up the underground rivers that fed the earth. It also would devour "the territory," or dry up the land allotted to Israel (v. 4). Here is a picture of a severe drought that God was ready to send on the land in judgment.

Again Amos interceded for Israel, pleading with God to stop this horrible plague: "Cease, I pray! Oh, that Jacob may stand, for he is small" (v. 5). God again answered the prophet's plea with a promise: "This also shall not be" (v. 6). Notice that God responds to His people's prayers to delay coming judgment.

The Fatal Vision

Then Amos received a third vision, that of a "plumb line" (v. 7). The Lord is pictured standing on a wall with a plumb line in His hand to determine the wall's vertical straightness (v. 7).

Israel had been plumbed correctly when originally forged into a nation (Ex. 19:7–8; 24:3, 7). But over the centuries, it had become unaligned with God's upright law. The Lord is portrayed as a surveyor measuring to what degree Israel is out of plumb (Amos 7:8). After proper testing, God had no alternative but to destroy Israel for being structurally unsound. The Lord told Amos that he need not intercede for Israel because His patience with the nation was exhausted. God would "not pass by them anymore," meaning He would not divert or delay the scheduled judgment (v. 8).

First, God would destroy Israel's religious structure: "The high places of Isaac shall be desolate, and the sanctuaries of Israel shall be laid waste" (v. 9). The pagan shrines in Bethel, Dan, and along the hillsides of Israel would be destroyed. Then He would destroy the nation's political structure: "I will rise with the sword against the house of Jeroboam" (v. 9).

Notice, Amos did not declare that King Jeroboam himself would perish by the sword but that his descendants would (cf. 2 Ki. 14:23–29). Jehu (in the line of Jeroboam I) was promised that his descendants would reign only four generations (2 Ki. 10:30). This prophecy was fulfilled when Shallum killed Zechariah, the son of Jeroboam II, severing the house of Jeroboam from Israel (15:8–10).

Someone has rightly said, "God's patience, long sinned against, will at length be sinned away." When God's patience is exhausted with a sinning nation, intercessory prayer on behalf of that nation is to no avail.

The Vision Mocked

When Amos spoke of Israel's religious and political destruction, he inflamed both Amaziah the priest and King Jeroboam, for the temple at Bethel was where Jeroboam II worshiped (Amos 7:10). More important, it was the religious symbol that inspired support for his dynasty. To denounce Bethel and its religious system was tantamount to attacking Jeroboam's reign (cf. 3:14; 4:4–5; 5:5–6, 21–26; 7:9; 9:1).[2]

Amaziah shrewdly responded by sending a delegation to the palace to charge Amos before the king. First, he charged Amos with conspiring to turn the people against Jeroboam (7:10). Second, he charged that Amos was plotting the king's death and Israel's captivity (v. 11). Third, he warned Jeroboam, "The land is not able to bear all his words" (v. 10). In other words, the people might believe Amos and revolt against the king. These charges all distorted Amos's message. Notice how Amaziah did not mention that Amos had called Israel to repent and turn from its religious apostasy. Neither did he mention the prophet's supplicating prayer for Israel's survival.

The king never acted on Amaziah's charges. Perhaps he did not feel threatened because of his power and political security. Perhaps he considered Amos a crackpot prophet. Perhaps he considered Amos a true prophet and feared to act against him. Or perhaps he did not want to stir up controversy in Israel. Whatever the case was, like many political leaders today, the king simply ignored God's messenger and message.

Upon receiving no consideration from the king, Amaziah confronted Amos personally. In a sarcastic tone, he advised Amos, "Go, you seer! Flee to the land of Judah. There eat bread, and there prophesy" (v. 12). The phrase *eat bread, and there prophesy* implied that Amos was a hireling prophet who made a living by selling his services (Mic. 3:5–11).[3] In reality, Amaziah was a hireling priest who projected his own lifestyle on Amos.

Amaziah commanded Amos to leave Bethel for two reasons. First, it was the "king's sanctuary," where only the king's prophets and priest could minister. Second, it was the king's "royal residence," where Amos had no right to be (Amos 7:13). In today's vernacular, Amaziah was saying, "Get out of here! You have no right to the king's city, altar, or house! Go back to Judah, and prophesy all you want at your own national altar!"

Amaziah exemplifies the many religious leaders who are spiritually blind and unable to recognize a messenger of God and the truth he brings.

Amos denied any standing as a professional prophet: "I was no prophet, nor was I a son of a prophet" (v. 14). It was God who had chosen and called Amos from the occupation of a "sheep-breeder and a tender [gatherer] of sycamore fruit" to prophesy against Israel (v. 14). As a sheep breeder, Amos probably had a side business of growing sycamore fruit in the Jordan Valley. The term *tender* (gatherer), refers to Amos climbing the sycamore tree and pinching the maturing fruit so it could ripen. In all likelihood, he was a rugged, outdoors type, quite different from the Israelite society to whom he was called to minister.

God had commissioned Amos while he was busily engaged in secular employment: "Then the LORD took me as I followed the flock, and the LORD said to me, 'Go, prophesy to My people Israel'" (v. 15). He had no recourse but to obey God's call, even though a corrupt priest like Amaziah might not like his message.

Amos did not seek the ministry; God had called him. Amos did not select his mission: "The LORD said to me, 'Go . . . to My people, Israel'" (v. 15). Amos did not speak his own message; he was given what God wanted Israel to hear: "Now . . . hear the word of the LORD" (v. 16). And Amos was not to fear man's opposition; he spoke boldly to Amaziah the priest (v. 17).

There is a parallel between Amos's call and that of the

apostles. The Lord called the apostles from secular employment and commanded them to take His message to the lost sheep of Israel. They, too, had to face opposition from Israel's high priest. They, too, were faithful in obeying God's commission to preach God's message. And they, too, did not allow the prohibition of the priests to keep them from doing the work God had called them to do (Acts 5:28–29).

The Vision Described

Since Amaziah had rebelled against God's prophecy, he would suffer four personal tragedies. First, his wife would become a prostitute, a "harlot in the city" where once she had held a position of prominence (v. 17).[4] As Amaziah had been unfaithful to the Lord, so his wife would be unfaithful to him. Second, his posterity would be killed: "Your sons and daughters shall fall by the sword" (v. 17). Amaziah's name would be cut off in Israel. Third, his property would be "divided by survey line" and given to foreigners. Fourth, the priest would "die in a defiled [unclean] land" (v. 17). He would be stripped of his priesthood and position and exiled to a foreign land where he would be engulfed in paganism until he died.

Had Israel heeded Amos's message, forsaken its idolatry, and turned to God, it would have been spared. But Israel ignored the prophet's message. Thus it would be "led away captive" (v. 17). God's patience had run its course and His judgment was ready to fall.

The United States should heed God's message to Israel through the prophet Amos. Our country was once a strong nation built on the principles of God's Word. But like Israel, it has drifted into the dark waters of decay and decadence. The degree of moral decline in America is shocking. Easy divorce, the breakdown of the nuclear family, abortion on demand, sexual immorality of every sort, acceptance of perverted art as a right of free expression, proliferation of illegal drugs, the court system's interpretation of laws in a way that harms godly causes—all these indicate where this country is headed. One need not be a prophet to predict the impact such trends will have on America's survival.

In November 1989 President George H. W. Bush predicted the 1990s would be a "decade of democracy" worldwide. Now, almost 20 years later, the world is worse than ever. The handwriting is on the wall. The world is on a collision course, as nations are being moved into place for end-times prophecy to be fulfilled.

God has been gracious in diverting and delaying judgment on America. But if repentance does not come soon, the cherished democracy that we have enjoyed for more than 200 years might soon become a dim memory.

CHAPTER 22

A DYING DYNASTY

In winter it is trendy to give friends large baskets of fresh fruit wrapped in cellophane and tied at the top with a red bow. The fruit is beautiful to look at, but if left in a warm room, it quickly discolors as decay sets in. What was once beautiful to see, succulent to taste, and fragrant to smell becomes repugnant and must be discarded. So has God portrayed the final days of Israel's great dynasty.

Israel's Destiny

Amos received a fourth vision where the Lord revealed the nation's collapse, comparing it to "a basket of summer fruit" (Amos 8:1–2). *Summer fruit* refers to a fully ripened crop that is ready for harvest and signals the end of the growing season in Israel. Thus Israel was fully ripe for God's judgment.

There is a play on the words with *summer fruit* (Hebrew, *qayis*) and *end* (Hebrew, *qes*) or "end time for cutting." Just as the produce had reached its time for being picking, so Israel had reached its time to be cut down in judgment.

How wrong President George H. W. Bush's "decade of democracy" declaration turned out to be. World leaders are becoming more belligerent every day. God has been gracious in diverting and delaying His judgment on America, but He will not wait forever. Judgment will catch up with us, just as it did with Israel.

The privileges God had bestowed on Israel were misused. Passionate invitations to repent went unheeded, and Amos's warnings met the same fate. God's mercy to Israel would soon cease: "The end has come upon My people Israel; I will not pass by them anymore" (v. 2).

Although harvest time is a joyful occasion, it would not be so for the Israelites. Their joyful songs of the Temple would be changed to wailing as they grieved over their national destruction (v. 3). A harvest of dead bodies would be gathered in every place for burial (cf. 5:3). Those delegated to bury the dead would be so overcome by the carnage that they would carry out their task in utter silence (8:3).

This picture is reminiscent of the Holocaust of World War II. Who has not seen pictures of half-dead, emaciated Jewish men limping along in stunned silence as they pushed toward a common grave rickety carts piled high with Jewish corpses? Anyone seeing such a scene for the first time is usually stunned into silence.

Israel's Deeds

Amos went on to describe the sins that made Israel ripe for judgment. First, dishonest businessmen had "swallow[ed] up the needy, and [made] the poor of the land fail" (v. 4). The words *swallow up* are better translated "to pant after," picturing the eagerness of these people to devour the poor as a wild beast devours its prey (cf. 2:6–7). These greedy profiteers targeted poverty-stricken, defenseless people and confiscated their meager holdings through harassment and intimidation. They would "buy the poor for silver, and the needy for a pair of sandals," meaning that those who were unable to pay their debts were sold into slavery for a little silver or the price of a pair of shoes (8:6).

Israel's business community was so greedy for wealth that it chafed under the law that required business to cease for the monthly observances of the new moon and weekly sabbath (v. 5). Most likely these people spent their time not in worship but in scheming new ways to accumulate greater profits when the markets reopened.

Second, these businesses used deceptive weights and measures, "making the ephah small and the shekel large, falsifying the scales by deceit" (v. 5). The *ephah* (bushel) used in measuring grain was made smaller, cheating the people out of grain. In addition, the shekel used to weigh money for purchase was made heavier to facilitate overcharging. So the scales were falsified; people did not receive the amount of grain they paid for, and they paid more than they should have for what they bought. God strongly condemned such evil.

Third, businessmen deprived people of the basic sustenance for good nutrition. They sold the poor the "bad wheat" that was of no value. It was unfit for human consumption and was usually thrown out or given to the poor (v. 6). But these profiteers mixed this material into the packages of grain they sold. Bible scholar Theo Laetsch pointed out, "Their insatiable lust for gold impelled them to resort to shamefully fraudulent tricks. Even the barest necessities of life, wheat and 'corn,' grain in general, were to them welcome means of squeezing profits out of the needy brethren."[1]

Such attitudes are prevalent in business today. Blue laws, instituted to prohibit Sunday commerce, have vanished in most communities. Sunday has become the most lucrative day of the week for most businesses in this country. The nation is replete with scams run by unscrupulous people who prey on the elderly and undiscerning to fleece them of their money.

Israel's Dark Days

Such injustices perpetrated on the poor could not go unpunished. God's heavenly judgment was about to be pronounced on Israel's leaders: "The LORD has sworn by the pride of Jacob: 'Surely I will never forget any of their works'" (v. 7). The Lord vowed He would never forget the extreme wickedness done to the poor in Israel. "Shall the land not tremble for this?" demanded the Lord (v. 8).

What did the prophet mean by the phrase *The LORD has sworn by the pride of Jacob?* Two interpretations are possible. Some believe God vowed *against* the "pride of Jacob"; that is, against the arrogant way in which Israel treated the poor and put its trust in wealth. Others believe the phrase refers to God Himself, who is Israel's pride and glory. Thus God swore by Himself that He would not forget the evil Israel had done to its poor. Most commentators hold the latter position.

Amos used three metaphors from nature to describe the

severity of God's judgment on Israel. First, it would be like an earthquake that causes the whole land to tremble, striking terror in the inhabitants (v. 8). Second, foreign armies would sweep across the land, spreading destruction as "the River of Egypt" (the Nile) does when it floods, rising and receding and spewing mire and debris everywhere. Third, God would "make the sun go down at noon, and . . . darken the earth in the broad daylight" (v. 9). Possibly Amos had a literal solar eclipse in mind, for two had taken place in his day (784 B.C. and 763 B.C.). More likely, however, he was picturing Israel enshrouded in the black mantle of God's judgment.[2]

This description is a clear picture of the Assyrian army invading Israel. The land would tremble under the horses' hooves as the army flooded into Israel, spreading death and destruction and bringing a dark day to Jeroboam's dynasty. The result of such devastation would cause everyone in the land to mourn (v. 8). Their joyful feasts would be turned into mourning; their joyful songs, into a lamentation (funeral dirge); their expensive clothing and beautiful coiffures, into "sackcloth . . . and baldness," signs of deep mourning over sin (v. 10). God would pierce them with the deepest grief possible, like the "mourning for an only son" who had died (v. 10). Such a loss meant the family name would die (Jer. 6:26; Zech. 12:10).

Most suffering and mourning soon cease or at least lessen over time. But not Israel's grief. Its mourning would be "like a bitter day" (Amos 8:10). It would not be a passing grief but an unending time of sorrow that would last as long as the Israelites lived. The image is that of an "undying death in hell!"[3]

Israel's Doom

The Lord had sent Israel His Word time and again, warning of coming judgment if the nation did not repent of its sin (2:11–12; 3:1; 4:1; 5:1; 7:10–13, 16). But Israel had tried to stop the prophetic voice sent to it. Its leaders commanded the prophet, "Do not prophesy" (2:12); "Go . . . to the land of Judah . . . and there prophesy. But never again prophesy at Bethel" (7:12–13). God's Word and warning had gone unheeded. Instead they had been despised, ignored, rejected, and trampled under foot.

So Israel was granted its desire. God withdrew His Word so that the nation would hear it no longer. He sent a "famine on the land, not a famine of bread, nor a thirst for water, but of hearing the words of the LORD" (8:11). He removed the prophetic voice from Israel.

Hunger to hear the Word of God would become so great that people would "wander [reel like a drunken man] . . . to and fro, seeking the word of the LORD" throughout the land (v. 12). Their search would take them "from sea to sea [the Mediterranean Sea to the Sea of Galilee], and from north to east" (v. 12). Notice that they did not seek God's Word in the south (Judea and Jerusalem) where it could be found. Their search was fruitless. God's Word was hidden from them. They "shall not find it," said Amos (v. 12).

Following Israel's destruction in 722 B.C., the prophetic voice could be heard only in Judah. The prophets continued to speak even to the exiles of Judah and then to the remnant returning from the Babylonian Captivity. Yet even in Judah there were long periods (690–650 B.C. and 492–437 B.C.) when no prophetic voice was heard in the land. Upon the completion of Malachi's prophecy (420 B.C.), there was no written or spoken word from God until John the Baptist broke the silence more than 400 years later.[4]

John's message told people to prepare for the Messiah's coming. Sadly, Israel's religious and political leaders rejected his message, too. But the greatest rejection came when Israel's leadership refused to receive the Word of God from Jesus, their Messiah. He came as spiritual bread and spiritual water to satisfy their need (Jn. 6:51; 7:37–39). After almost 2,000 years, the nation is still experiencing spiritual famine.

But there is a spiritual famine among many Gentile nations as well. For more than 70 years, people living under Communist rule were deprived of God's Word. Happily, this situation is beginning to change. Yet there are millions of people in India and in Muslim countries the world over who are starving for spiritual truth because their leaders and their religious beliefs have kept the Bible from them.

Although the United States possesses more Bibles than any country in the world, there is a growing famine when it comes to reading God's Word. Carnal Christians, who feed on self-indulgence, have lost their taste for reading the Bible. Secularism, greed, and immorality have so inundated America that most people have no appetite or tolerance for God's Word.

God's harsh judgment took its toll on "the fair virgins and strong young men" of Israel, those who were hearty and should have been able to endure hardship because of their youth (Amos 8:13). Even they would "faint from thirst"—physical thirst, to be sure, but also spiritual thirst because they were unable to hear God's Word (cf. v. 11). During those dark days, the young people would feel helpless concerning the future. They would need a word from God to bring spiritual healing and hope; but God would be silent. If hearty youths would faint under this calamity, what would happen to babies and the elderly? Most assuredly, few would survive this tragic day of doom.

The Pilgrims who settled America built the Ivy League colleges primarily to train young people in the Word of God with the purpose of evangelizing the Atlantic seaboard. Harvard, Yale, and Princeton all had godly beginnings. Harvard's motto, adopted in 1692, was "Veritas Christo et Ecclesiae," Latin for "Truth for Christ and the Church." Even today the phrase can be found on many of Harvard's buildings. Harvard's *Rules and Precepts*, adopted in 1646, states, "Let every Student be plainly instructed, and earnestly pressed to consider well, the maine [main] end of his life and studies is, to know God and Jesus Christ which is eternal life (John 17:3). . . . Every one [sic] shall so exercise himselfe [sic] in reading the Scriptures twice a day."[5]

How different is the educational system in America today. God has been expelled from our schools, and the state has replaced Him with a secular "savior" called humanism. The new savior has bankrupted our young people, leaving them bereft of God's Word and, therefore, with no moral compass for the future. Most churches and families are not much better at providing spiritual food for a starving generation of young people.

The Israelites should have lived by God's Word. Yet they did not and were severely judged for their continual practice of idolatry: "Those who swear by the sin of Samaria, who say, 'As your god lives, O Dan!' and, 'As the way of Beersheba lives!' They shall fall and never rise again" (Amos 8:14). In other words, they worshiped the golden calves at Bethel and Dan and made the 140-mile pilgrimage to Beersheba to commit idolatry (Dt. 9:21; 1 Ki. 12:28–30; 2 Ki. 10:29; Hos. 8:5–6). Amos made it clear that Israel's idolatrous practices had sealed its doom: "They shall fall and never rise again" (Amos 8:14).

Israel had been God's vineyard. He had cultivated it, cleared out the stones, planted it with the choicest of vines, built a tower to oversee its development, and prepared a winepress to process the beautiful harvest He expected to receive. But Israel produced only wild grapes. Disheartened over the fruit, the Lord laid waste to His vineyard. He took away the hedge, broke down the fences, withheld rain, and did not cultivate or prune it. In time it was ruined, and the residue was trampled under foot (Isa. 5:1–7). What a sad commentary on the people of God!

America, like Israel, was forged into a strong nation by the sovereign hand of Almighty God. No other nation in history has experienced such freedom, majesty, and blessing. But this fruitful nation is showing signs of spoilage. Sin has so discolored and decayed the moral fabric of this country that many see America as a dying democracy in the 21st century. Let us take to heart God's message to Israel and pray that our nation will rise up in revival before it falls, never to rise again.

CHAPTER 23

A NATION OF DESTINY

Israel is an enigma to the world. The nation was miraculously created from the loins of a married couple long past the age of childbearing. It was endowed with divine privileges and covenant promises, enabling it to enjoy a spiritual position unparalleled in the annals of human history. During its early history, it was protected from neighboring nations bent on its annihilation.

In time, however, tragedy befell Israel. The nation perverted and prostituted its spiritual privileges, bringing God's judgment. God turned Israel's glory into gloom as the nation suffered national destruction and dispossession of its land and was dispersed worldwide, becoming the tail rather than the head of all nations. It wandered from country to country, where it was scorned, abused, and defamed.[1]

Yet this people resisted assimilation and annihilation by the nations to which it was driven. Like the fabled phoenix, Israel rose from the ashes of destruction and is again planted in its land, as predicted by the prophets.

In his final message to Israel, Amos picked up his prophetic brush one last time and, in broad strokes, painted this scenario of Israel's history. He began his message with the theme of his prophecy, alerting Israel to God's soon-coming judgment.

Revelation Provided to Israel

In his fifth vision, Amos saw the image of a judge, "the Lord standing by the altar" (Amos 9:1). The word *Lord* is not the covenant name Jehovah, but *Adonai*, denoting, as Dr. Laetsch put it, "the God of absolute authority and power to do as He pleases with His subjects."[2]

Where is the altar on which the Lord is standing? Some believe it to be in Solomon's Temple; thus the prophet's message would be to both Israel and Judah. Others teach the altar is in Israel only, most likely the royal altar of Jeroboam. The context of this passage supports the latter view.

The altar was to be a place where God provided mercy through substitutionary sacrifice; but when the altar has been defiled and the sacrifice despised, it becomes a place of judgment only.[3]

The Lord is pictured bringing idolatry to judgment. He smote "the doorposts, that the thresholds may shake," causing the Temple roof to collapse, which in turn resulted in the Temple's destruction (9:1). The scene is reminiscent of Samson's destruction of the Philistine temple dedicated to the pagan god Dagon. Samson pulled down the two center pillars that supported the roof (Jud. 16:23–30).

Amos spoke of an inescapable judgment. Those who were not killed when the Temple collapsed would be decapitated by the invading Assyrian army. None would escape, for the Lord would "slay the last of them" (v. 1).

God's judgment would be inescapable because He is omniscient and omnipresent. Although some would try to escape by digging "into hell" (*sheol*, meaning the lowest depth possible), God would find them (v. 2). Although some would try to "climb up to heaven" (meaning the greatest height possible), God would find them and "bring them down" (v. 2). Although they would try to hide in the rugged, wooded area of Carmel, which is filled with many caves, God would find them (v. 3). Although they would hide "at the bottom of the sea," God would send a serpent (sea monster) to "bite" (kill) them (v. 3). And though they would be willing to go into captivity like submissive sheep, hoping to preserve their lives, they would be slain even in their slavery (cf. Lev. 26; Dt. 28).[4] Thus Israel would be unable to escape judgment, for God had set His "eyes on them for harm and not for good" (Amos 9:4; cf. Dt. 28:63; 2 Chr. 16:9; Ps. 34:15; Jer. 24:6).

The Lord's judgment was inescapable because He also is omnipotent. His finger play brings havoc to the earth. God can touch "the earth and it melts, and . . . swell[s] like the River" (Amos 9:5).

In other words, God can flatten the land by earthquakes, melt the rocks by pouring burning lava over the land, and bring floods at His will. Such instability in the earth terrifies some, causing them to mourn. Others are killed by these natural catastrophes, such as those drowned by "the River of Egypt" (v. 5).

This great God controls the universe:

He who builds His layers [stairs to His throne] in the sky, and has founded His strata [vaulted dome, or the arch of heavenly planets] in the earth; who calls for the waters of the sea, and pours them out on the face of the earth—the LORD *is His name* (v. 6).

Amos pictured the Lord as a great God who created and controls heaven and earth, knits them together, and keeps them functioning with perfect balance. Thus the omnipotent, omniscient, omnipresent God who accomplishes all these things is not the calf-idol of Bethel to whom Jeroboam II sacrificed, but the Lord: "The LORD is His name" (v. 6).

Retribution Poured on Israel

God has selected Israel and given it more privileges, promises, and prosperity than any other nation. But this privileged position would not save it from judgment. In fact, God would treat Israel like the Ethiopians, a foreign people living in obscurity without God or hope in this world and totally despised by Israel (v. 7). Such would be God's attitude toward Israel because of its sin.

God had sovereignly delivered Israel from the land of Egypt and brought it into the Promised Land of Canaan. But this action was not unique, for He had brought "the Philistines from Caphtor [possibly Crete], and the Syrians from Kir [somewhere in Mesopotamia]" (v. 7). Although these nations were not as privileged as Israel, God had judged the Philistines and the Syrians for their sins (1:3–6). So would He destroy Israel and send it into captivity for rebelling against Him.

Israel had totally surrendered to sin: "The eyes of the Lord GOD are on the sinful kingdom," Amos declared. And He was about to allow the northern kingdom to be destroyed "from the face of the earth" (v. 8). Although God permitted the Assyrians to level Israel in 722 B.C., He still showed the Israelites mercy in the midst of judgment because He promised, "I will not utterly destroy the house of Jacob" (v. 8).

Yet God would "sift" Israel because of its sin: "I will command, and will sift the house of Israel among all nations, as grain is sifted in a sieve; yet not the smallest grain shall fall to the ground" (v. 9). God was about to scatter the Jewish people around the world, and they would suffer during centuries of exile. As grain is sifted to separate it from worthless chaff and other impurities, God would use this purifying process to protect and spare Israel. Israel has indeed been sifted throughout the nations for some 19 centuries, as satanically obsessed leaders have attempted to destroy the Jewish people.

In A.D. 135, the Roman Emperor Hadrian took over Jerusalem and persecuted the Jews. He posted edicts against the practice of Judaism, and any infringement brought the death penalty. Jews were barred from Jerusalem; those trying to enter the city were killed. During the first crusade in 1096, Jews were branded as enemies of Christendom, and 12,000 were killed along the Rhine River in Germany. In 1181, King Phillip of France banished the Jewish people from his country, stripping them of their land and houses. In 1189, at the coronation of Richard the Lionhearted, persecution resulted in most Jewish houses in London being burned and Jewish people being murdered. Then the Crown claimed their possessions.

In 1348, the Jewish people were blamed for the Black Plague of Europe and were slaughtered. In Germany alone, almost 12,000 Jewish people were killed. In 1478, the Spanish Inquisition broke out; and in 1492, about 300,000 Jews were banished from Spain and many more killed. In 1520, they were banished from Naples, Genoa, and Venice, Italy. In 1794 Jews were restricted in Russia, and Jewish men were forced to serve 25 years in the Russian army. By 1903, renewed restrictions were levied against the Jewish people, and frequent pogroms (massacres) broke out as the Russians destroyed many Jewish villages.

The worst holocaust to come on the Jewish people took place between 1933 and 1945 when 6 million died at the hands of Hitler's Nazis, as he cruelly and systematically superintended over the destruction of European Jewry.

Yet, despite all of this suffering, the Jewish people have

survived—in fulfillment of Amos's amazing prophetic forecast.

Amos warned that some would be punished because of their rebellious attitudes: "All the sinners of My people shall die by the sword, who say, 'The calamity shall not overtake nor confront us'" (Amos 9:10). Amos was saying that those who falsely boasted that judgment would not fall on the nation would be purged out by death (6:1–3, 13).

Jeremiah prophesied Israel's survival in the midst of severe judgment. And although God might make a full end of all the nations to which He would scatter His people, He promised He would not make a full end of Israel (Jer. 30:11). In fact, He promised that Israel would survive as long as the earth existed (31:35–38). What a marvelous promise of God's grace and mercy in the midst of extreme judgment!

Restoration Promised to Israel

Amid the doom and destruction, a glimmer of hope shines: Israel will again possess its land. Amos prophesied, "On that day I [God] will raise up the tabernacle of David, which has fallen down" (Amos 9:11). The words *on that day* had been used to describe Israel's judgment (2:16; 3:14; 5:18–20; 8:3, 9, 11, 13). But now Amos used these words to proclaim the nation's restoration, spiritual reunion, and redemption.

The word *tabernacle* refers to the royal house of David, which the Lord has established forever in the Davidic Covenant (2 Sam. 7:11–16). Sin brought the Davidic dynasty to decay and decline, making it only a shadow of its once-great power. With the destruction of Judah in 586 B.C., the rule of the house of David ceased (Jer. 22:24–30).

However, when the Messiah returns to set up His Kingdom, the Davidic Kingdom will be reestablished (Ezek. 37:24–25). "On that day," said the Lord, "I will raise up the tabernacle of David, which has fallen down, and repair its damages [i.e. the city wall]; I will raise up its ruins [rebuild Israel], and rebuild it as in the days of old [days of Solomon]" (Amos 9:11).

Then Israel's boundaries will be expanded to include all the land promised to Abraham (Gen. 15:18). Israel will possess the "remnant of Edom, and all the Gentiles who are called by My name," meaning the surrounding nations who trust in the Lord

(Amos 9:12). These nations will enjoy the Messiah's blessing and protection along with Israel. Israel has not known peace with its Gentile neighbors over the centuries, but in that day it will have peace because the Lord will accomplish it (v. 12).

The apostle James quoted this passage at the Jerusalem Council to show that Gentiles who accepted Christ did not have to undergo circumcision and become Jewish proselytes (Acts 15:14–17). In quoting Amos, James proved to the Council that Jewish and Gentile believers would exist side by side during the Kingdom Age.

Therefore, during the Church Age, there is no need for Gentiles to become Jews.

During the Kingdom Age many changes will take place in the land of Israel and throughout the world. First, the land will become extremely productive, as "the plowman shall overtake the reaper, and the treader of grapes him who sows seed" (Amos 9:13). In that day drought and famine will be replaced with a proliferation of produce (1:2; 4:6–8). "The mountains shall drip with sweet [new] wine, and all the hills shall flow with it" (9:13). The vines will be so loaded with mature grapes that their juices will drip on the mountainside while the grapes wait to be harvested, giving the appearance that the mountains are melting.

Second, Jewish people will return from their captivity (v. 14). They will experience an unprecedented peace as they are reinstated in their land to rebuild their destroyed cities (v. 14). Such peace will enable them to plant vineyards and enjoy the fruit of their labors in the Kingdom Age (v. 14).

Third, Amos assured Israel that He will plant the nation in its land permanently: "'I will plant them in their land, and no longer shall they be pulled up from the land I have given them,' says the LORD your God" (v. 15). This glorious promise to Israel is a guarantee from the Lord that its possession of the land is to be permanent.

Some Christians deny that God has promised to reestablish Israel physically in the land of Canaan and fulfill the covenant promises He made to Abraham and his seed. They believe the promises to Israel were conditioned on the nation's obedience to God; and since Israel sinned, breaking its agreement with God, it forfeited God's promise of a literal reestablishment. Those holding this position teach that the church has replaced Israel, and the promises made to the nation are now being fulfilled spiritually in the church. Thus the church is the "true" Israel of God today, known as spiritual Israel.

This interpretation contains several insurmountable problems. First, it is clear from Scripture that the promises to Abraham and his seed were given unconditionally and eternally; they did not depend on Abraham's faith or obedience for their fulfillment (Gen. 12:1–3; 15:7–8; 16:6–8). Second, Scripture never states that the church has replaced Israel and become spiritual Israel. Third, nowhere in the Bible is it said that Israel has forfeited its right to enjoy the promises given in the Abrahamic, Davidic, and New Covenants. In fact, the opposite is true. Over and over again, God gives Israel assurances in the prophetic writings that He will fulfill His covenant promises to the nation. Those who deny this position do not interpret Scripture literally. They spiritualize the text and, in so doing, erroneously interpret the passages dealing with Kingdom promises to Israel.

What an exciting day we live in, as we witness God beginning to fulfill His promises to Israel! He is breaking the chains of Israel's captivity and gathering Jews from worldwide dispersion, as predicted centuries ago by Israel's prophets (Dt. 30:3–5; Isa. 11:11–12; Ezek. 36:24; 37:4–14). More than 1 million Russian and Eastern European Jews have returned to Israel since Communism was dissolved.

Israel is being raised from the ashes of destruction to fulfill its destiny. The cities have been rebuilt, desolate land is being revitalized, and vineyards are producing in abundance—a miracle in our time, to be sure.

An unknown poet captured the spirit of the prophecy in this final chapter of the book of Amos when he penned,

Scattered by God's avenging hand,
Afflicted and bemoaned.
Sad wanderers from their pleasant land,
The Jew has now come home!

INTRODUCTION TO MICAH

Micah was a country prophet from Moresheth Gath (Mic. 1:1, 14). The name Micah is a short form of Micaiah and means "who is like Jehovah." Nothing is known of his family background or occupation. He had a deep compassion for the poor and a courageous spirit and spoke boldly concerning the moral corruption, hypocritical religious practices, and political suppression of his day.

Micah was a contemporary of Isaiah and prophesied to the southern kingdom of Judah during the reigns of Jotham, Ahaz, and Hezekiah (1:1). He also wrote in the style of Isaiah, using poetic parallelisms and many puns, probing questions, and figures of speech.

During the reign of King Uzziah (792–740 B.C.), Judah became very prosperous. And along with prosperity came social, political, and religious corruption. Uzziah was succeeded by his son Jotham (750–731 B.C.) who turned out to be a good king but who failed to cleanse Judah of its idolatry. Upon his death, Ahaz (735–715 B.C.) became king of Judah. He was extremely wicked and practiced Baal worship. An alliance between Israel (King Pekah) and Syria (King Rezin) threatened to topple Ahaz because he would not join them to oppose Tiglath-Pileser III, king of Assyria (745–727 B.C.). Instead, Ahaz joined Tiglath-Pileser III to overthrow the coalition of Syria and Israel. This was a bad move for Ahaz because, in the process, Judah became a vassal to Tiglath-Pileser III who required King Ahaz to pay him tribute.

Upon Ahaz's death, Hezekiah took the throne of Judah (715–686 B.C.) and proved to be one of the best kings in the nation's history. While Hezekiah ruled, Sargon II (722–705 B.C.) ruled Assyria and manifested extreme cruelty toward those nations under his control. He was succeeded by Sennacherib (704–681 B.C.). Judah, along with other nations, revolted against Assyria, prompting Sennacherib to invade Judah in 701 B.C. Hezekiah was surrounded by Sennacherib's Assyrian army. Though the kingdom's destruction seemed inevitable, God supernaturally delivered Judah from Sennacherib's forces (2 Ki. 18—19).

Although Hezekiah brought religious reforms to Judah, Judah's worship of God was merely an outward show to acquire divine favor (2 Chr. 29—31; Mic. 3:11; 6:6–8). Idolatry and even human sacrifice continued throughout the land. Judah's prophets and priests were corrupt, hiring out their services to the highest bidder (Mic. 2:11). The rich rulers oppressed the poor morally and socially (2:1–2, 8–9). In violation of the 10th Commandment, they confiscated land that was to be a permanent possession of the poor (Ex. 20:17; Lev. 25:10, 13). The rulers perverted justice and practiced gross iniquity, judges took bribes, and businessmen cheated their clients (Mic. 3:1–3, 9; 6:11; 7:3). The social, moral, and religious scene could be summed up with the following phrase: *A man's enemies are the men of his own household* (7:6).

A number of Micah's prophecies have been fulfilled, and others are yet to be fulfilled. The fulfilled ones include the destruction of Samaria (1:6–7); Assyrian invasion of Judah (vv. 9–16); destruction of Jerusalem and Solomon's Temple (3:12; 7:13); Babylonian Captivity (4:10); return and restoration of Judah (vv. 1–8, 13; 7:11, 14); and the Messiah's tribe, birthplace, and eternality (5:2). Micah also prophesied the Messiah's future reign, which has yet to be fulfilled (2:12–13; 4:1, 7).

Judging by the kings under whose reign he lived, Micah's prophecy can be dated between 750–685 B.C. (1:1) The moral, social, and religious corruption spoken of took place during Jotham's and Ahaz's reigns, but not after the reforms of Hezekiah (1:5; 2:1–13). The prophecy of Samaria's destruction had to come before 722 B.C. (1:6). Thus Micah probably issued his prophecy in stages between 735 and 710 B.C.

Micah's prophecy was intended to denounce the moral, social, and religious sins of Judah's leaders and to speak out against injustices to the poor. Micah was a champion of righteousness, especially for the poor. He heralded the message that judgment and captivity were coming soon, but he coupled it with a message of hope that the Messiah would appear. Thus the theme of Micah is the judgment and future restoration of Judah and Israel. Key verses are 1:5–6, 9; 3:9–12; 4:1–4; 5:1–2; 7:18–20. Key words are *desolation* (mentioned four times) and *gather* (used nine times).

ᵛ

OUTLINE OF MICAH*

I. Judgment Predicted (chaps. 1—2)
  A. Prediction of Judgment (1:1–16)
    1. God's Faithful Witness (1:1–5)
    2. God's Fierce Wrath (1:6–16)
  B. Purpose of Judgment (2:1–13)
    1. Princes of Sin (2:1–3)
    2. Parable of Sorrow (2:4–5)
    3. Prophets' Sin (2:6–11)
    4. Promised Survival (2:12–13)

II. Justice Promised (chaps. 3—5)
  A. Rebuke before the Kingdom (3:1–12)
    1. Princes' Corruption (3:1–4)
    2. Prophets' Carnality (3:5–7)
    3. Prophet's Confidence (3:8)
    4. Pollution of the City (3:9–11)
    5. Pronouncement of Collapse (3:12)
  B. Restoration of the Kingdom (4:1—5:1)
    1. Renewal Prophesied (4:1–5)
    2. Regathering the People (4:6–8)
    3. Remembering the Past (4:9–10)
    4. Retaliation Predicted (4:11–13)
  C. Return of the King (5:2–15)
    1. Revealing the Messiah (5:1–2)
    2. Rejection by the Messiah (5:3a)
    3. Return of the Messiah (5:3b)
    4. Rule of the Messiah (5:4–15)

III. Jehovah's Prosecution and Pardon (6:1—7:20)
  A. Prosecution Revealed (6:1–5)
    1. The Call (6:1–2)
    2. The Controversy (6:3–5)
  B. Purity Required (6:6–8)
    1. Rhetorical Inquiry (6:6–7)
    2. Righteous Individuals (6:8)
  C. Prosperity Repudiated (6:9–12)

1. Instruments of Wrath (6:9)
2. Ill-gotten Wealth (6:10)
3. Irregular Weights (6:11)
4. Israel's Wickedness (6:12)
D. Punishment Rendered (6:13–16)
 1. Sickness Results (6:13)
 2. Satisfaction Removed (6:14a)
 3. Storehouse Rifled (6:14b)
 4. Sowing Without Reaping (6:15)
 5. Sins Repudiated (6:16)
E. Prophetic Remorse (7:1–6)
 1. Prophet's Sorrow (7:1–2)
 2. People's Sins (7:3–6)
F. Pleading for Restoration (7:7–13)
 1. Confidence in the Lord (7:7–8)
 2. Confession to the Lord (7:9)
 3. Conviction in other Lands (7:10)
 4. Comfort From the Lord (7:11–13)
G. Prayer for Redemption (7:14)
H. Promise From the Redeemer (7:15–17)
 1. Strength of the Lord (7:15)
 2. Silence Before the Lord (7:16)
 3. Surrender to the Lord (7:17)
IV. Pardon of the Remnant (7:18–20)
 1. Patience of God (7:18)
 2. Pity From God (7:19a)
 3. Protection of God (7:19b)
 4. Pardon From God (7:19c)
 5. Promise to the Godly (7:20)

*Outline does not always follow chapter titles or outline in each chapter.

CHAPTER 24

A WARNING TO JUDAH

One of the brightest and yet darkest periods of Judah's history came in the eighth century B.C. Although the prosperity of Uzziah's kingdom (792–740 B.C.) was still being felt in the days of his son Jotham (750–731 B.C.), along with it came social, political, and religious corruption. Rich rulers oppressed the poor, perverted justice, and practiced gross iniquity; and judges and businessmen were dishonest and unethical.

Into this defiled setting, "The word of the LORD . . . came to Micah of Moresheth in the days of Jotham, Ahaz, and Hezekiah, kings of Judah" (Mic. 1:1). Although Micah wrote to both Israel and Judah, his message was primarily to Judah. Moresheth Gath was located on the border of Judah, about six miles from Lachish.

Ahaz (735–715 B.C.) succeeded Jotham as king of Judah. His reign proved to be among the worst in Judah's history. Ahaz was one of Judah's evil kings, and his wickedness brought God's judgment. After Ahaz, his son Hezekiah became king (715–686 B.C.). Hezekiah was a blessing to Judah and proved to be one of the best kings in the nation's history. When the Assyrians, under King Sennacherib, threatened to destroy Jerusalem in 701 B.C., Hezekiah prayed; and God supernaturally delivered Judah and Jerusalem from destruction (2 Ki. 18—19).

Unfortunately, Judah's worship of God was mere conformity to a prescribed ritual and ceremony. Prophet and priest alike were corrupt, and they sold their services for profit. Micah tried to convince Judah that external religious ritual must be accompanied by principles of righteous conduct if the nation was to please God.

The prophet said he "saw" ("came to") the "word of the LORD," meaning he received an inner, prophetic revelation concerning Samaria and Jerusalem (Mic. 1:1). In chapter 1, Micah used Samaria's impending destruction as a wakeup call to Judah. If Jerusalem's repentance were not forthcoming, it would suffer the same fate as Samaria.

God's Faithful Witness

All nations were summoned to hear the coming judgment of God:

> *Hear, all you peoples! Listen, O earth, and all that is in it! Let the Lord GOD be a witness against you, the Lord from His holy temple. For behold, the LORD is coming out of His place; He will come down and tread on the high places of the earth. The mountains will melt under Him, and the valleys will split like wax before the fire, like waters poured down a steep place* (vv. 2–4).

The one testifying against the nations is none other than the "Lord GOD" who is enthroned in heaven. He alone will bear witness against the nations' sins. God will step out of His holy sanctuary and descend to Earth like a mighty, victorious warrior to execute the prophesied judgment. He will tread on the "the high places" where both Israel and Judah practiced idolatry—a prediction of Assyria's invasion of Samaria in 722 B.C. and the Babylonians' invasion of Judah in 586 B.C. The picture of mountains melting and valleys splitting in verse 4 symbolizes the awesome power and terror the Lord's judgment will produce, foreshadowing the Great Tribulation when the Lord will judge the nations.

God's judicial verdict resulted from Israel's sin: "All this is for the transgression of Jacob and for the sins of the house of Israel. What is the transgression of Jacob? Is it not Samaria? And what are the high places of Judah? Are they not Jerusalem?" (v. 5).

The term *Jacob* refers to all 12 tribes of Israel, whose father is Jacob. Iniquity filled all the land because both the northern kingdom of Israel and southern kingdom of Judah embraced Canaanite Baal worship. The negatively posed questions expect a positive answer, underscoring why God manifested His wrath and judgment against Israel and Judah. Because of Israel's gross idolatry, God destroyed Samaria:

176

Therefore I will make Samaria a heap of ruins in the field, places for planting a vineyard; I will pour down her stones into the valley, and I will uncover her foundations. All her carved images shall be beaten to pieces, and all her pay as a harlot shall be burned with the fire; all her idols I will lay desolate, for she gathered it from the pay of a harlot, and they shall return to the pay of a harlot (vv. 6–7).

In plain language that Judah could understand, God promised the destruction of Samaria that took place in 722 B.C. First, Samaria will look like a heap of stones on the side of a field cleared for planting a vineyard. Second, so thorough will be Samaria's destruction that even its foundation will be torn down. Third, all its idols will be melted; and the gold, silver, and offerings people gave in religious prostitution will be offered to the idols in Assyria. The picture was a vivid warning to Judah, which had become like Israel in its worship. Micah lamented God's revelation:

Therefore I will wail and howl, I will go stripped and naked; I will make a wailing like the jackals and a mourning like the ostriches, for her wounds are incurable. For it has come to Judah; it has come to the gate of My people—to Jerusalem (vv. 8–9).

The prophet walked throughout the land, clothed only in a loincloth, crying out in mournful tones that sounded similar to the haunting cry of a jackal and fearful screech of an ostrich. Judah's wound will be incurable, reaching the very gates of Jerusalem. Micah's lament is presented in a prophetic perfect; that is, it speaks of a future judgment as if it had already happened.

God's Fierce Wrath

What follows is a list of the cities that Assyria will invade on the way to Judah. Micah used the name of each city as a play on words in describing the destruction. He used a word that sounds like the name of the city or comes from the city's name to describe its demise. First, "Tell it not in Gath, weep not at all" (v. 10). The name Gath sounds similar to the Hebrew word for "tell." That is, "In tell town, tell it not." Micah did not want the people of Gath in Philistia to hear about the Assyrian attack on

Judah so that the Philistines would not rejoice on hearing the news. Micah exhorted the Israelites not to show sorrow because it would give comfort to their enemy.

Second, "In Beth Aphrah [house of dust], roll yourself in the dust" (v. 10). Rolling in dust symbolizes sorrow, shame, humiliation, and intense mourning.

Third, "Pass by in naked shame, you inhabitant of Shaphir" (v. 11). *Shaphir* means "beautiful." The city would be denuded of its beauty and grace by experiencing shameful treatment during captivity.

Fourth, "The inhabitant of Zaanan ["going forth"] does not go out," or did not stir to come out of the city and fight because of the strength of the Assyrian army (v. 11).

Fifth, "Beth Ezel ["place nearby"] mourns; its place to stand is taken away from you" (v. 11). The death wails of Beth Ezel will scare off those who seek shelter or protection from the Assyrian invasion.

Sixth, "For the inhabitant of Maroth ["bitterness"] pined [waited anxiously] for good, but disaster came down from the LORD to the gate of Jerusalem" (v. 12). Maroth will taste the bitterness of destruction, not deliverance, because the Lord will send calamity all the way to Jerusalem.

Seventh, "O inhabitant of Lachish, harness the chariot to the swift steeds (She was the beginning of sin to the daughter of Zion), for the transgressions of Israel were found in you" (v. 13). Micah sarcastically urged the people of Lachish to harness their horses quickly in order to flee the Assyrians; but they will not escape judgment, because they had introduced Baal worship to Judah and Jerusalem.

Eighth, Judah will be required to "give presents to Moresheth Gath" (v. 14). *Moresheth* sounds like *meorasah*, meaning "betrothed." The word *presents* is used for the dowry given to a daughter when she marries. (See 1 Kings 9:16.) Judah must give, as a present to the Assyrians, the city once betrothed to it.

Ninth, "The houses of Achzib [literally, "deception"] shall be a lie to the kings of Israel" (v. 14). Achzib will defect to the attacking Assyrians and be lost as a city to which the kings of Judah can flee for defense.

Tenth, "I will yet bring an heir to you, O inhabitant of

Mareshah" (v. 15). The Hebrew word *Mareshah* sounds like the word *inheritance*. Micah was saying that the Lord will bring an inheritor (King Sargon) who will claim Mareshah as his inheritance.

Eleventh, "The glory of Israel shall come to Adullam" (v. 15). Adullam once provided protection for King David as he fled from Saul (1 Sam. 22:1–2). In like manner, Judah's royalty will try to flee to Adullam to escape the Assyrian invasion.

In verse 16, Micah concluded his lament by calling on Judah to make itself bald in the day of its captivity, a pagan practice forbidden by Jewish law but adopted by Judah on the death of a near relative (Lev. 19:27–28; Dt. 14:1; Amos 8:10). Judah's great desolation will make the kingdom feel like a mother mourning the death of her "precious children" (literally, "the children of thy delight"; Mic. 1:16). They were to "enlarge [their] baldness like an eagle" (v. 16). When the bald eagle molts, it looks more or less bald and appears sickly and aged. The Judeans will mourn because their children "shall go from you into captivity" (v. 16). The exile mentioned here is most likely the Babylonian Captivity of 586 B.C., when the Babylonians destroyed Jerusalem and Solomon's Temple, not the Assyrian captivity mentioned in verse 10.

When disaster is imminent, a nation and its leaders need to be like Micah who lamented before the Lord over his people's sin and pleaded to God for mercy as well as deliverance. May we heed this admonition as well.

CHAPTER 25

JUDAH'S CORRUPT LEADERS

God gave the Jewish people the land of Canaan as an everlasting inheritance. However, their uninterrupted possession of it was conditioned on the nation walking in God's ways and keeping His commandments. Failure to do so would result in Israel's temporary removal from the land (Lev. 20:22). Throughout its history, Israel broke all of God's commandments, and both Judah and Israel lost the land of their inheritance.

In Judah's society, abuse of the Mosaic Law was graphically illustrated by the deeds of the elite who misused the poor. These affluent and influential men illegally appropriated the property of the less fortunate and sold their holdings, such as livestock, for unpaid debts. Their control of the legal system stripped the poor of their rights. And no one spoke out against these injustices except the prophets in Judah.

Micah was well aware that the wealthy were preying on the poor. The prophet called these rich rulers to account for how they oppressed the downtrodden, perverted justice, and destroyed the moral and social fabric of the nation. The court scene presented in chapter 1 continues in chapter 2. God finds these rich rulers guilty of criminal acts against the poor and pronounces judgment on the nation.

The Poor Defrauded

Micah began his message by condemning the deeds of the wicked:

Woe to those who devise iniquity, and work out evil on their beds! At morning light they practice it, because it is in the power of their hand. They covet fields and take them by violence, also houses, and seize them. So they oppress a man and his house, a man and his inheritance (2:1–2).

The word *woe* is a pronouncement of guilt and a threat or imprecation from the Lord concerning the calamity about to befall the wealthy for their abuse of the poor. Affluent landlords coveted the peasants' land that joined their estates. These wicked men lay awake all night, carefully devising well-engineered plans to acquire wealth at the expense of the poor through manipulating the country's legal system. If that did not work, they seized property by brute force.

Crooks usually cover their felonies under the shroud of darkness; but these sharks perpetrated their crimes during the morning court sessions. These powerful landlords used slick lawyers who perverted justice by finding loopholes in Judah's legal system. They so tightly controlled the courts that the poor had no right of appeal on the judicial decisions handed down.

Upon entering the land of Canaan, every Israelite received a portion of land. Owning land provided a man with freedom and a livelihood and brought civility and stability to Israel's society. If a peasant was deprived of land in this agrarian society, he became a day laborer at best and a slave at worst. Property surrendered for debt was never to be kept forever but was to be returned to the original owner in the year of jubilee (Lev. 25:13). Confiscating a man's land with no intention of ever returning it defied the divine principle of inheritance set forth in the Mosaic Law (Dt. 19:14).

The Lord declared through the prophet, "Behold, against this family I am devising disaster [a calamity], from which you cannot remove your necks; nor shall you walk haughtily, for this is an evil time" (Mic. 2:3). Notice that God disowned them as His people by calling them "this family." As these wicked landlords had devised evil against the poor, God would devise evil to befall them. Humiliation and the iron yoke of judgment will replace the pride of Judah's affluent. They had oppressed their brethren; now they will experience the same fate.

In the day of judgment, the mourner will chant a doleful parable of lamentation and say, "We are utterly destroyed! He has changed the heritage of my people; how He has removed it from me! To a turncoat He has divided our fields" (v. 4). In their distress, the rich landlords will cry out like the poor whom they had defrauded and victimized. As they had defrauded the poor of their land, so their land will be permanently stripped from them and confiscated by the conquering heathen. There is no indication they cried out in repentance, only in remorse, on losing their land to a heathen nation.

These covetous landlords will receive the same treatment they inflicted on the poor. "Therefore," said Micah, "you will have no one to determine boundaries by lot in the assembly of the LORD" (2:5). In short, these unscrupulous landlords will have no one to measure an allotment of land to them as Joshua did when he divided land among the tribes of Israel (Josh. 14:1–2). Because they blatantly oppressed the poor, they will be permanently cut off from any inheritance within Judah and will have no part in a future restoration to the land.

The Prophet Denounced

The covetous landlords and false prophets commanded Micah to stop prophesying because he preached truth that revealed their corruption: "'Do not prattle', you say to those who prophesy. So they shall not prophesy to you; they shall not return insult for insult [disgrace]" (Mic. 2:6). The words translated "Do not prattle" are from *natap,* a Hebrew word that means "to drip." In other words, these men were telling Micah, "Stop dripping irritating words of condemnation on us." The prohibition against prophesying is immediately followed by another form of *natap* that is translated "those who prophesy." They were commanding Micah to stop prattling on about threats of judgment because his forecast of shame and disgrace (so they claimed) would not come true for Judah.

Micah was considered a dangerous agitator because his pointed prophecy disgraced the landlords and embarrassed the false prophets who foretold only peace and prosperity. These men believed that as long as Micah's "impertinent," "irrelevant," and "inappropriate" prophesying continued, they would be humiliated and disgraced in the public eye.

Micah answered his critics by asking three rhetorical questions concerning their ongoing complaint: "[1] You who are named the house of Jacob: 'Is the Spirit of the LORD restricted [less long-suffering]? [2] Are these His doings? [3] Do not My words do good to him who walks uprightly?" (v. 7).

These landlords and false prophets boasted that they were the chosen people of God, descendants of Jacob, men with whom God was pleased for their faith and obedience. But Micah told them they had ceased to be anything like their father Jacob. They were wrong to imagine that God was no longer long-suffering toward His Chosen People because He announced judgment on Judah. God has always been and still is long-suffering. These men also had reasoned that, if God is long-suffering and He promised blessing through Jacob their forefather, how can judgment be "His doings"(v. 7)? In their minds, Micah was wrong to characterize God as a God of wrath and vengeance who punishes His people.

But they held erroneous views of God's character. Judgment is not out of character with God's nature. In fact, God as a Father would be remiss if He did not discipline His disobedient children. Micah's third rhetorical question, "Do not My words do good to him who walks uprightly?" received a positive answer. God's words are, in fact, good and prove to be a blessing, not a threat, to the upright.

Micah pointed out that these princes of Judah were committing acts of injustice at the time of his prophecy: "Lately [literally, "yesterday"] My people have risen up as an enemy" (v. 8). In short, the leaders of Judah had committed recent and repeatedly blatant acts of violence and oppression against society; and by so doing, they became the Lord's enemy, provoking Him to judgment.

In the preceding verses, Micah provided concrete examples of how Judah's leaders were enemies of God. First, they "pull off the robe with the garment from those who trust you, as they pass by, like men returned from war" (v. 8). These leaders acted like soldiers returning from a battle with the belief they had the right to ambush unsuspecting and innocent people. They stripped them of their belongings, especially their expensive outer robes and inner garments (tunics)—necessities of life. The law prohibited a creditor from keeping a man's garment overnight, even if it was taken in a pledge (Ex. 22:26). Second, Judah's leaders abused women (probably widows) and their children by confiscating their homes and evicting them from their property (Mic. 2:9). This deprived these children of the Lord's glory forever, meaning the privileges due them under the Mosaic Law.

These rich landlords had stripped others of their inheritances as well. Now they themselves will be removed from the land of their rest and heritages. Through Micah, God ordered the people to rise and depart from Judah. Because the leaders had defiled the land with their despicable deeds, the land will vomit them out. Eventually, they will be removed from Judah through death or captivity (v. 10).

Micah continued: "If a man should walk in a false spirit and speak a lie, saying, 'I will prophesy to you of wine and drink,' even he would be the prattler of this people" (v. 11). In other words, these rich leaders accepted the message of the false prophets who predicted affluence and prosperity, but they totally rejected Micah's message of impending judgment.

The Promise Declared

Micah abruptly changed the tone of his message in verse 12 from one of judgment to a promise of deliverance. First, the restoration spoken of here pictures a greater fulfillment than Judah's deliverance from its 70-year captivity in Babylon. The prophecy looks forward to a day when the Messiah will gather and restore all saved Jews and lead them into the Promised Land at the beginning of the Millennial Kingdom. Second, He will gather them in great numbers like "the sheep of the fold [Bozrah]," an area in Edom known for rearing great flocks of sheep. Third, the Jewish people will return to the land "like a flock in the midst of their pasture," or to a productive field that will provide for all its needs. Fourth, the throngs of returnees will be so great that the sound and shout of their rejoicing over salvation will echo throughout the pasturelands like "so many people."

Micah closed this portion of his prophecy by introducing the Deliverer of Israel who is called "the one who breaks open [the breaker]" (v. 13). The term *breaker* is a Messianic title and refers to the time when the Messiah will deliver Israel from its enemies during the "time of Jacob's trouble": the Great Tribulation (Jer. 30:7). Shepherds function as breakers when they remove a wall, hedge, or other obstacle that would impede their sheep from passing through a gate to pasture. In like manner, the Messiah will break open the way; remove every obstacle in Israel's path; and go before the nation as its King, leading the redeemed through the gate to Kingdom blessing (Mic. 2:13). Though Judah faced judgment, a future, glorious day of deliverance still awaits.

CHAPTER 26

MICAH'S CALL FOR JUSTICE

In the book of Micah, God holds Judah's leaders responsible and accountable for their abuse of the underprivileged. Earlier, Micah condemned those who used the nation's legal system to defraud people of their property. However, in chapter 3, Micah more fully described Judah's corruption, denounced the civil and religious leaders' wickedness, and announced the imminence of divine judgment.

Corrupt Politicians

Micah began with a call for leaders to hear God's message: "Hear now, O heads of Jacob, and you rulers of the house of Israel: Is it not for you to know justice?" (Mic. 3:1). The names Jacob and Israel refer to the southern kingdom of Judah because Assyria already had destroyed the northern kingdom. It is these "heads" and "rulers" of Judah whom Micah condemned, those who were responsible for maintaining order and justice in Judah's national life—political leaders, civic governors, judges, tribal elders, and military officials. God had appointed these men to ensure justice.

The prophet's rhetorical question, "Is it not for you to know justice?" expects a positive response. It was mandatory for all Judah's rulers and leaders, especially judges, to know the Mosaic Law and adjudicate using God's standards of right and wrong (Dt. 1:13–17). Such was not the case. The judges were unprincipled men who had long forsaken the Mosaic standard of justice for new, dishonest laws that benefited their evil agendas.

Micah described these men as follows: They "hate good and

love evil" (Mic. 3:2). They no longer made judicial decisions based on what was right and good; but, loving evil, they aided and abetted the criminals in Judean society for their own greedy, selfish gain. The description of their wickedness becomes even more intense:

> *[They] who strip the skin from My people, and the flesh from their bones; who also eat the flesh of My people, flay their skin from them, break their bones, and chop them in pieces like meat for the pot, like flesh in the caldron* (vv. 2–3).

Judah's leaders were like starving, wild animals that unconscionably, savagely, and unmercifully grab their prey, rip open its skin, and gorge themselves on the animal's flesh and blood. So thorough were these butchers that they consumed their victims as cooks who chop the meat and grind the bones of an animal they are going to boil in a pot. These tyrannical leaders were heartless and cruel and totally consumed every possession their victims owned.

The use of such grotesque metaphors emphasized the deep depravity of these inhumane rulers who should have been the guardians of justice, guarantors of human rights, and protectors of Judean society. Instead, they abused their positions and used brutal lawlessness to satisfy their greed for power, property, and possessions. God calls the prey of these ungodly rulers "My people," a term of endearment used to depict the Lord's loving relationship with His covenant people Israel (v. 3).

Micah said a day will come when the tables will be turned, and these lawless rulers will cry out fervently to God for mercy in their hour of need: "Then they will cry to the LORD, but He will not hear them; He will even hide His face from them at that time, because they have been evil in their deeds" (v. 4).

These profane men had lived and functioned as if there were no God to whom they must give account. Those who showed no mercy to the people of Judah and turned a deaf ear to their cries will receive the same treatment they meted out. God will hide His face from them and refuse to hear the cries of their anguish. He will be silent to their pleas and show them no grace or mercy.

Covetous Prophets

The second group that God condemns is that of the false prophets:

Thus says the LORD concerning the prophets who make my people stray; who chant "Peace" while they chew with their teeth, but who prepare war against him (v. 5).

The people looked to these perverted prophets as men who knew the mind of God and, in so knowing, would direct the nation properly. Instead, these pseudo prophets deliberately misled Judah for their own selfish and greedy ends. God condemns such people and puts them under a divine curse (Dt. 27:18).

The phrase *chew with their teeth* has been interpreted two ways. Some believe the verse teaches these false prophets predicted peace and prosperity only when they received food or material goods in return. Others believe it speaks about these men's lying words, which inflicted harm like the bite of a serpent. Both teachings are true. These false prophets spoke of peace and prosperity to those who provided for them monetarily or materially. But to someone who gave nothing, they prepared, or sanctified, "war against him"; that is, they predicted a curse.

Therefore, Micah declared, "You shall have night without vision, and you shall have darkness without divination; the sun shall go down on the prophets, and the day shall be dark for them" (Mic. 3:6).

God's judgment will descend on these charlatans like *night* and *darkness*, words that depict these people's impending destruction. God will not give them visions or answers to explain their calamity. Nor will these prophets say they have visions from the God of peace and prosperity. And in the day of their calamity, these prophets no longer will seek answers to their dilemma by using divination (magic and spiritism). The sun will set on their prosperity—and on any possibility of deliverance (v. 6).

In that day, "the seers shall be ashamed, and the diviners abashed; indeed they shall all cover their lips; for there is no answer from God" (v. 7). Men who looked to these prophets for direction and illumination concerning the future will disown them and put them to public shame. These prophets will be "abashed," or struck dumb, because their prophetic gift will be stripped from them. In humiliation, they will "cover their lips" (v. 7). Covering the outer lip (including the face) was a sign of embarrassment, shame, and mourning (Lev. 13:45). Covering their mouths was an appropriate sign that they had nothing to say. If, perhaps, they sought God for a remedy to their predicament, they would receive no answer. God will remain silent and provide no revelation. It would seem that these prophets did possess a true gift from God; but over time, they prostituted it for financial gain.

In contrast to the powerlessness of the pseudo prophets, Micah's power was from God. He told the people, "But truly I am full of power by the Spirit of the LORD, and of justice and might, to declare to Jacob his transgression and to Israel his sin" (Mic. 3:8). Micah stated three facts about his power and authority: (1) He was filled by the power of the Holy Spirit to speak God's Word; (2) his words of justice or righteous judgment were not his own and came directly from God; and (3) he was given might, or manly courage, to stand against men fearlessly and preach boldly against the sins of "Jacob" and "Israel" (the entire nation, cf. 3:1, 9).

Condemning Prophecy

A scathing recapitulation of the sins of Judah's rulers and religious leaders follows in verse 9. The prophet denounced their false confidence in believing that the Lord would not allow calamity to come on them. These men, who were to be the upholders of justice, in reality "abhor [despise] justice and pervert [twist] all equity" (v. 9). They despised justice and twisted and distorted the facts of each case that came before Judah's courts. Those accused in a lawsuit could never be assured a fair verdict unless they bribed the judge.

These leaders "build up Zion with bloodshed and Jerusalem with iniquity" (v. 10). That is, the means of building Jerusalem was through extortion by the wealthy at the expense of the poor. Jerusalem's buildings and palaces were built with blood money gained by fraud, confiscation of property, and even murder. The entire justice system was utterly corrupt.

Civil and religious leaders performed their duties with an eye on getting wealthy: "Her [the nation's] heads judge for a bribe, her priests teach for pay, and her prophets divine for money" (v. 11). Judicial decisions were predicated on who provided the largest bribes. God established the priests to teach; interpret the Law; and decide questions on religion and ritual, free of charge (Dt. 17:8–11). But they only did so for financial gain. And He established the prophets, whom Micah already had denounced, to provide revelation from God gratuitously. But they used demonic divination and charged for it (cf. Balaam, Num. 23—24).

Micah continued: "Yet they lean [support themselves] on the LORD, and say, 'Is not the LORD among us? No harm can come upon us'" (Mic. 3:11). These corrupt leaders believed they had immunity from God's judgment because (1) they were in a covenant relationship with Him; (2) God's Shekinah glory was present in the Holy of Holies; and (3) they practiced Judaism by offering the required animal sacrifices at specified times, in obedience to the Lord. For these reasons, they erroneously believed He would safeguard them from destruction.

How mistaken these men were. Their gross immorality and hypocritical religious practices made God's judgment of them inevitable: "Therefore because of you Zion shall be plowed like a field, Jerusalem shall become heaps of ruins, and the mountain of the temple like the bare hills of the forest" (v. 12).

"Because of you" or because of the leaders' sins, three events will befall Jerusalem. First, Zion will be completely destroyed and become a leveled field for plowing and planting seed. Second, Jerusalem will be torn down and left in ruins. Third, the Temple Mount will become overgrown with trees, briars, and thorns.

King Hezekiah took Micah's prophecy to heart. He humbled himself, repented of sin, and brought religious and social reforms to Judah (Jer. 26:17–19). Because Judah turned to God, destruction was postponed for more than a century.

Micah's message is certainly a word from God for our time. The economic, political, religious, and moral situation in America is not unlike Judah's. People skirt or break laws for greed, material gain, or to drive up stock prices. Politicians take advantage of legal loopholes to gain political advantage or fatten their campaign coffers. Americans worship at the feet of materialism and technology during the week and give God lip service in church on Sunday, with little or no commitment. The nation needs to heed Micah's message before it suffers the same fate as Judah.

CHAPTER 27

A FUTURE HOPE FOR ISRAEL

Many questions must have troubled King Hezekiah and the leaders of Judah when they heard Micah preach of the nation's impending demise. After all, if Judah were destroyed, how would God fulfill the irrevocable promises He had made to the children of Israel in the Abrahamic and Davidic Covenants?

In this chapter, God gives the people of Judah hope and assurance. He has not forgotten His promises to their forefathers. Although Judah will be destroyed, God will again redeem a remnant from under the iron heel of Gentile oppression and reestablish the nation in its Promised Land. This event will take place when the Messiah comes to rule the world from David's throne.

Renewal

Micah shifted abruptly from his predictions of doom to give Judah hope of renewal and restoration "in the latter days" (Mic. 4:1). The phrase *the latter days* refers to when Jewish people will undergo great tribulation, followed by Christ's Second Coming to restore the nation and establish Jerusalem as the center of His divine rule on Earth. Moses had prophesied this tribulation and restoration before Israel entered Canaan (Dt. 4:25–31).

Micah's prophecy includes six predictions affecting Israel. First, "the mountain of the LORD's house shall be established on the top of the mountains, and shall be exalted above the hills" (Mic. 4:1). The mountains surrounding Jerusalem are higher than Mount Moriah, where the Temple once stood. At Messiah's return all the mountains surrounding Jerusalem will be flattened

(Zech. 14:4). Jerusalem, as well as the Temple Mount, will become elevated above the surrounding area.

Second, Israel and the nations of the world will worship in Jerusalem, "and peoples shall flow to it. Many nations shall come and say, 'Come, and let us go up to the mountain of the LORD, to the house of the God of Jacob'" (Mic. 4:1–2). During the Millennial Kingdom, all roads will lead to Israel as people from the nations of the world encourage one another to go up to worship in Jerusalem at the Millennial Temple.

Third, saved Gentiles the world over will be taught by the Lord at the Temple in Jerusalem: "'He will teach us His ways, and we shall walk in His paths.' For out of Zion the law shall go forth, and the word of the LORD from Jerusalem" (v. 2). Revelation on how to live a righteous life and keep the Lord's commandments will be provided to a new generation.

Fourth, nations will bring their disputes to Jerusalem for the Lord to arbitrate:

He shall judge between many peoples, and rebuke strong nations afar off; they shall beat their swords into plowshares, and their spears into pruning hooks; nation shall not lift up sword against nation, neither shall they learn war anymore (v. 3).

The Lord will settle all disputes, war will be eliminated, and this difficult and grasping world will finally know true peace. Nations will turn their weapons into farm implements and will cease teaching their people the strategies of war.

Fifth, with the elimination of war, nations will live in safety and security: "But everyone shall sit under his vine and under his fig tree, and no one shall make them afraid" (v. 4). During King Solomon's reign, the words *vine* and *fig tree* were associated with peace, plenty, and prosperity (1 Ki. 4:25). The same will be true during the Millennial Kingdom because "the mouth of the LORD of hosts has spoken" (Mic. 4:4). No one will need fear an aggressive act from his neighbor because the Lord God Almighty, the omnipotent Head of the armies of heaven, has guaranteed peace.

Sixth, idolatry will be gone: "For all people [will (literally, "now")] walk each in the name of his god, but we will walk in the name of the LORD our God forever and ever" (v. 5). In Micah's day, all heathen nations ordered their lifestyles and religious beliefs after false gods. But a godly remnant in Judah ordered its conduct according to the Lord. In the future Kingdom, Judah will continue to put total trust in the Lord, while the nations of the world will put away their heathen gods and follow the Lord.

Regathering

"In that day," says the LORD, *"I will assemble the lame, I will gather the outcast and those whom I have afflicted; I will make the lame a remnant, and the outcast a strong nation; so the* LORD *will reign over them in Mount Zion from now on, even forever"* (vv. 6–7).

The prophet did not say when this prophecy will be fulfilled. The word *remnant* cannot refer to the Jewish people who returned from the Babylonian Captivity because the Lord did not reign over Judah "forever." The words *in that day* must refer to the Millennium, when the Messiah will rule over Israel forever. The remnant of Israel that will be restored is compared to a flock of sheep that were "lame" (footsore), sick, afflicted, and dispersed—a picture of Israel's condition during the Great Tribulation. Afterward, at the beginning of the Millennium, God will regenerate and restore one-third of the previous Jewish population—all who survive the Great Tribulation (Zech. 13:9). When the Messiah returns, this remnant will have the veil of unbelief lifted from its eyes and come to salvation (Zech. 12:10; Rom. 11:26).

In keeping with the metaphor of sheep, Micah used a circumlocution to express Jerusalem's elevation when the Messiah comes to rule during the Millennium: "And you, O tower of the flock, the stronghold [Hebrew, *ophel*] of the daughter of Zion, to you shall it come, even the former dominion shall come, the kingdom of the daughter of Jerusalem" (Mic. 4:8).

The phrase *O tower of the flock, the stronghold of the daughter of Zion* refers to the southernmost section of the Temple Mount, opposite Zion, separated by the Tyropoeon Valley. The words *tower* and *ophel* are used synonymously of the strongholds in the City of David, later fortified by Jotham and Manasseh (2 Chr.

27:3; 33:14). It was the place where David's palace once stood and where the king's men stood as watchmen over the people of Jerusalem. When the Messiah returns to Jerusalem, He will restore the daughter of Zion to her "former dominion" and guarantee Israel protection, peace, political power, and prosperity (Mic. 4:8). The picture is reminiscent of the Davidic and Solomonic empires, which were strong, stable, and impervious to attacks from other nations. This prophecy gave hope to a nation that would soon suffer the pain of destruction and captivity.

Remembering

Micah abruptly switched tracks to predict again the destruction and captivity of Judah. The prophet asked three rhetorical questions concerning the time of the Babylonian siege: "Now why do you cry aloud? Is there no king in your midst? Has your counselor perished? For pangs have seized you like a woman in labor" (v. 9). In other words, why did great wailing break out in Judah? Did they not have a king and counselor to call on for help during the Babylon threat? Yes, they had kings; but the kings were powerless to lead the nation or counsel it during the Babylonian siege. Jehoiakim and Zedekiah each reigned when Babylon occupied Judah; but both served Nebuchadnezzar, king of Babylon (2 Ki. 24—25).

After Babylon destroyed Judah, the children of Israel were left without a king; and they will remain so until the time of their redemption (Hos. 3:4–5). Without leadership, pain and agony would grip the nation as birth pangs grip women in labor. Although the reference is to the Babylonian Captivity, the situation will be the same during "the time of Jacob's trouble" (Jer. 30:5–7; Rev. 12), the Great Tribulation. Micah continued:

> Be in pain, and labor to bring forth, O daughter of Zion, like a woman in birth pangs. For now you shall go forth from the city, you shall dwell in the field, and to Babylon you shall go. There you shall be delivered; there the LORD will redeem you from the hand of your enemies (4:10).

Judah's captivity is pictured in stages. As the people of Judah are compelled to leave the city, they will cry out in panic like a woman suffering agonizing birth pains. On their forced march to

Babylon, they will be made to "dwell in the field," unprotected from the elements and predators. Multitudes will perish. After arriving at Babylon, the Judean remnant will be held in captivity for 70 years (Jer. 25:11). And at the end of 70 years, a remnant will be redeemed, or allowed to return, to Judah. This latter prophecy was fulfilled by edict of Persia's King Cyrus in 538 B.C. (Ezra 1:2–4). Micah's naming of Babylon is an amazing prediction in itself, for it came more than 100 years before all of Judah ended up there (Isa. 39).

Retaliation

In the future, heathen armies will trample Jerusalem's holy sites without pity: "Now also many nations have gathered against you, who say, 'Let her be defiled, and let our eye look upon Zion'" (Mic. 4:11). The world will gloat with glee over Israel's shame, suffering, and subjugation (cf. Dt. 28:37). This prophecy's ultimate fulfillment will come during the Great Tribulation.

Someday the nations will storm against Jerusalem, ignorant of what God has planned for them: "But they do not know the thoughts of the LORD, nor do they understand His counsel; for He will gather them like sheaves to the threshing floor" (Mic. 4:12). As sheaves are bundled and brought to the threshing floor to be trodden under the feet of oxen, so the nations that come against Israel will be destroyed. The annihilation they had planned for Israel will come on their own heads, especially during the Tribulation.

In verse 13 God directs Jerusalem to rise up and tread on its enemies as an ox treads out grain with his hoof. A horn of iron and hooves of bronze symbolize the power and strength the Lord will give Israel to fight its enemies. This event likely takes place when the Messiah comes to destroy the nations at the Battle of Armageddon (Rev. 16:16; 19:19). Then Israel will gather the wealth of the world and devote it to the Lord, whose power will have accomplished the victory. The phrase *to the Lord of the whole earth* refers to the Messiah (Christ) when He returns as "KING OF KINGS AND LORD OF LORDS" (Rev. 19:16; cf. Ps. 2:8–9).

Micah prophesied a message of hope to the household of Judah. But before this hope is realized, Judah must be punished for its disobedience to the Lord. In the future, Israel will experience a glorious victory over its enemies and enjoy redemption through its Messiah. Then Jerusalem will be exalted as the capital of the world.

CHAPTER 28

THE MESSIANIC KING AND HIS KINGDOM

For centuries, Jewish people have looked for the Messiah to deliver them from Gentile oppression, secure for them the land of Israel, rebuild the Temple on its historical site, and bring peace to Israel and the world.

Twenty-five centuries ago the Jewish prophets sketched the details of the Messiah's life and work. He is the only Person in history whose lineage, birth, character, teaching, career, reception, rejection, death, burial, and resurrection were recorded at least 500 years before His birth. One prophet who foretold the Messiah's coming was Micah. In chapter 5, Micah provided a number of marvelous prophecies about the Messiah from His birth to His Second Coming when He will establish the Millennial Kingdom.

Messiah Revealed

Micah wrote, "Now gather yourself in troops, O daughter of troops; he has laid siege against us; they will strike the judge of Israel with a rod on the cheek" (5:1). The phrase *gather yourself in troops* is a call to marshal groups of marauding troops within the city of Jerusalem to defend against a coming siege. The word *now* seems to describe an attack that is about to begin against Jerusalem, but it is unclear exactly when the attack will occur. Some believe it refers to the Assyrian assault under Sennacherib, mentioned in chapter 4. Others believe the siege is that of Babylon. Still others believe the prophet speaks of a siege against Jerusalem during the Tribulation before Israel is victorious over its foes at Christ's Second Coming. The context seems to speak of the Babylonian siege against Jerusalem in 586 B.C., which foreshadows a future siege against Jerusalem during the Great Tribulation.

The invaders will "strike the judge of Israel with a rod on the cheek" (v. 1). Smiting someone on the cheek signified great dishonor, insult, and humiliation to a ruler in that day. Some teach that the ruler being struck is Christ being hit on the head and face at His trial (Mt. 27:30; Jn. 19:3)). However, this position is not tenable. There was no siege on Jerusalem when Christ was crucified. The word *judge* (meaning "ruler") in verse 1 is a different Hebrew word from the word *ruler* in verse 2. The phrase *now gather* suggests this event will occur relatively soon, not centuries in the future. The text does not reveal the judge's identity but probably refers to King Zedekiah, who was tortured by the Babylonians when Nebuchadnezzar's soldiers invaded Jerusalem (2 Ki. 25:4–7).

Micah turned abruptly from the secular ruler of Jerusalem to predict the coming of a totally different King who will transcend human rulers. The Person Micah revealed in 5:2 is none other than the Messiah, who was to be born in Bethlehem Ephrathah. Almost 750 years later, scribes made the identity of the Ruler clear when King Herod gathered them together and "inquired [demanded] of them where the Christ [meaning Messiah] was to be born" (Mt. 2:4). They answered, "In Bethlehem of Judea, for thus it is written by the prophet" (Mt. 2:5). Then they quoted Micah 5:2:

> But you, Bethlehem Ephrathah, though you are little among the thousands of Judah, yet out of you shall come forth to Me the One to be Ruler in Israel, whose goings forth are from of old, from everlasting.

Throughout the first century A.D. it was commonly held that the Messiah would be a descendant of David, born in Bethlehem of Judea (Jn. 7:42).

A more amazing prophecy than the location of His birth is that His "goings forth are from of old, from everlasting [eternity]" (Mic. 5:2). This One, like God, is eternal. The word *everlasting* means "infinite" or "timeless in duration" and refers to the Messiah's eternality. This prophecy clearly states that Messiah's existence predates the universe's creation. God the Son became the God-man when He was born of the virgin Mary in Bethlehem of Judea (cf. Isa. 9:6; Jn. 1:1, 14). He will become the Ruler over Israel during the Millennium (Lk. 1:27–33).

Micah went on to reveal that God will "give them up [abandon Israel], until the time that she who is in labor has given birth; then the remnant of His brethren shall return to [with] the children of Israel" (Mic. 5:3). Judah's spiritual pain at being abandoned by God is similar to a woman's physical pain in childbirth. She agonizes in pain until the birth of her child; but afterward, the pain of childbirth is replaced with joy. Micah did not reveal when or how these events would take place.

Some believe this verse refers to Judah being subdued by foreign countries between the time Babylon smote the nation until Mary travailed in childbirth at the Messiah's First Advent. The verse does not refer to Israel's deliverance at Messiah's birth because, after that event, Judah was again "led away captive into all nations. And Jerusalem will be trampled by Gentiles until the times of the Gentiles are fulfilled" (Lk. 21:24).

Others believe Micah 5:3 refers to the time of Messiah's rejection at His First Coming until Israel's regathering at Messiah's Second Coming. This position is more plausible because Israel has been persecuted and dominated by Gentiles since A.D. 70 and is yet to undergo its greatest time of suffering during the Great Tribulation (Jer. 30:5–7). At that time Israel's suffering will be like the birth pains of a woman; but after the delivery will come joy. A remnant in Israel will go through the affliction of the Great Tribulation, experience regeneration at the Messiah's Second Coming, and then be regathered to enjoy Kingdom blessings.

Messiah's Reign

Messiah will shepherd Israel. In 5:4, Micah described the Lord's Messianic reign. He shall "stand" as Ruler in the Millennial Kingdom and will "feed" (shepherd) the restored remnant of Israel. Like a shepherd, He will lead, protect, and tenderly care for His people "in the majesty of the name of the LORD." His rule will manifest "the majesty," or the heavenly glory and power, of

Jehovah on Earth. Israel "shall abide," or dwell, in the land safely and securely, in perpetuity and prosperity. Messiah's rule will not be over Israel alone but will "be great to the ends of the earth" because He is King and Sovereign Lord over the entire world.

Messiah will subdue Israel's enemies. "And this One [the Messiah previously described] shall be peace. When the Assyrian comes into our land . . ." (v. 5). After His Second Coming, the Messiah, who is the Prince of Peace (Isa. 9:6), will be the Source of peace that covers the earth. The "Assyrian" is not the Assyria that invaded Judah in 701 B.C. but a symbol for future invaders who come against Israel in the Great Tribulation. When the invaders attack, "seven shepherds [those guarding the people] and eight princely men [princes or leaders]" will be ample enough (along with the coming Messiah) to repel the attack, for God will give them unusual strength to overcome their enemies.

"They shall waste with the sword the land of Assyria, and the land of Nimrod at its entrances [gates or strongholds of the cities]" (Mic. 5:6). Nimrod founded the kingdom of Babel (Gen. 10:10). But the "land of Nimrod" symbolizes the entire Babylonian-Assyrian empire. In the final analysis, it will not be Israel's leaders who deliver the nation at the end of the Great Tribulation, but the Messiah (Christ) "when he treads within our [Israel's] borders" to destroy its enemies (Mic. 5:6; cf. Zech. 14:3; Rev. 19:15).

A remnant of saved Jewish people will survive the Great Tribulation and will become a blessing to the Gentiles in the Millennial Kingdom: "Then the remnant of Jacob shall be in the midst of many peoples, like dew from the LORD, like showers on the grass" (Mic. 5:7). Restored Israel will bring continual spiritual blessings to the nations as dew and showers refresh the ground after a long dry spell.

In the Millennium this saved Jewish remnant will be feared. It will be "like a young lion among flocks of sheep, who . . . treads down and tears in pieces, and none can deliver" (v. 8). As a lion strikes fear in the animal kingdom when on the prowl, so Israel will dominate, exert power, and destroy all who oppose it. Whenever Israel will confront an enemy in the Kingdom, the Lord's hand will strike down the enemy, and "all your [Israel's] enemies shall be cut off" (v. 9).

Messiah will guarantee Israel's security. The Lord will destroy everything Israel relied on in the past for protection. He will destroy its armaments and accoutrements of war: "I will cut off your horses . . . and destroy your chariots. I will cut off the cities of your land and . . . all your strongholds" (vv. 10–11). In a peaceful world, Israel will not need horses, chariots, or fortified cities. All these means of defense will be superfluous because the Lord will be in the midst of Israel to defend it and guarantee its security.

Messiah will purge Israel of sorcery and sacred statues. The Lord will destroy the nation's "sorceries," "soothsayers [divination]," "carved images," and "sacred pillars [stones]." The Lord promises, "You shall no more worship the work of your hands; I will pluck your wooden images [Asherah poles used in sensual fertility rites]" (vv. 12–14).

For centuries Israel sought spiritual direction through witchcraft and occult practices that included magic and demonic involvement. Often these methods were used to acquire information from demonic sources to curse an individual or nation. Israelites had gone to soothsayers or fortune-tellers who claimed to predict the future. Before Israel entered the Promised Land, God forbade the nation to engage in such practices (Ex. 20:4; Lev. 19:31; Dt. 16:21–22; 18:10–12). With the destruction of idolatry, the Jewish people will no longer worship the work of their hands, but only the true and living God who redeemed them.

Messiah will require total submission to His sovereign rule. "And I will execute vengeance in anger and fury on the nations that have not heard" (Mic. 5:15). The Messiah will execute judgment on any individual or nation that defies His sovereign rule. During the Millennium, the Lord will rule with a "rod of iron" (Ps. 2:9; Rev. 12:5; 19:15). He will immediately put down any insurrection against His authority and punish those who do not obey Him.

What a tremendous blessing there will be when the Messiah returns. With a redeemed remnant restored to Israel and the Messiah ruling on Earth, the entire world will be blessed with peace and prosperity. Then the long-awaited promises God made to Abraham and David through the covenants will be completely fulfilled for Israel.

CHAPTER 29

GOD'S JUDGMENT AGAINST JUDAH

In chapter six of Micah, God brings litigation against the people of Judah, charging them with gross immorality and idolatry. Judah is the defendant, and the Lord is both the prosecuting attorney and judge.

Prosecution Revealed

As the proceedings open, Micah states the Lord's position:

Hear now what the LORD says: "Arise, plead your case before the mountains, and let the hills hear your voice. Hear, O you mountains, the LORD's complaint, and you strong foundations of the earth; for the LORD has a complaint against His people, and He will contend [plead] with Israel" (6:1–2).

Judah is asked to testify of any evil the Lord has committed against it. The mountains, hills, and foundations of the earth represent immutable and inanimate creation, which have, since time immemorial, stood in silent witness to God's gracious faithfulness toward evil Judah. They are asked to listen to God's lawsuit as He pleads with Judah concerning its sin and idolatry.

God asks Judah two rhetorical questions, requesting that the nation present any charge it has against Him: "O My people, what have I done to you? And how have I wearied you? Testify against me" (v. 3).

Judah is addressed as "My people," revealing God's strong covenant love, deep affection, and care for the nation. Like a father before his wayward son, God examined His own heart to see if He put unreasonable demands on Judah or neglected it, causing its unfaithfulness. In what way had He wearied Judah? Had He made harsh demands on it that were too difficult for the people to keep? Had He not provided enough help during its pilgrimage as a nation? Had He failed it during times of crises and conflicts?

Since Judah presented no countercharges, God answered His own rhetorical questions:

> For I brought you up from the land of Egypt, I redeemed you from the house of bondage; and I sent before you Moses, Aaron, and Miriam. O My people, remember now what Balak king of Moab counseled, and what Balaam the son of Beor answered him, from Acacia Grove to Gilgal, that you may know the righteousness of the LORD (vv. 4–5).

In short, God (1) liberated the Israelites from Pharaoh; (2) redeemed them from slavery in Egypt; (3) gave them Moses, Aaron, and Miriam as political and religious leaders to guide them; (4) delivered them from Balak's evil plan to curse them (Num. 22—24); and (5) took away their shame, providing forgiving grace at Shittim (Num. 25; Josh. 3:1).

It was at Gilgal, where Israel camped after entering the Promised Land, that God renewed His covenant (Josh. 4:19). There, through circumcision—the sign of being under the Abrahamic Covenant—God renewed His covenant promises and blessings with Israel and gave the nation strength to defeat its enemies (5:2–11). All these acts of grace and mercy were bestowed on Israel so that she "may know the righteousness of the LORD" (Mic. 6:5).

Judah, to whom God addressed His rhetorical questions and illustrations, knew it had no grounds for criticism or counter-charges against the Lord. Its unfaithfulness was not because of anything God did or did not do but was totally of its own making.

Purity Required

Israel responded to God's indictment by asking rhetorical, hypothetical questions. Micah presented Israel's questions in the first person singular, requesting that God give evidence of what

He required of individual Israelites. Some scholars believe these questions are querulous in tone, revealing Israel's deplorable ignorance. If not, they at least betray the nation's bankrupt spiritual condition. Other scholars believe these questions counter God's indictment of Israel and show Israel's willingness to give all to be restored to Him.

The Israelite asked, "With what shall I come before the LORD, and bow myself before the High God? Shall I come before Him with burnt offerings, with calves a year old?" (v. 6). He was asking what sacrifice God required him to bring in worship, so he could please God. If God would reveal His demands, the Israelite was ready in his devotion to present the type of sacrifice that would satisfy the Lord. The burnt offering, unlike other offerings, required that the entire animal be presented as a sacrifice. A 1-year-old calf was more valuable than a younger calf because time and expense had been invested in the animal.

Next, the Israelite asked how many sacrifices God required to please Him: "Will the LORD be pleased with thousands of rams, ten thousand rivers of oil?" (v. 7). Thousands of rams, great in value, were the offerings of a king like Solomon. God never required such a sacrifice from an individual. Or would God be pleased with a libation of ten thousand rivers of oil? Oil was presented in small amounts when the daily meal offering and other sacrifices were presented.

Israel's questions reach a crescendo with an absurd and unthinkable question: "Shall I give my firstborn for my transgression, the fruit of my body for the sin of my soul?" (v. 7). Such questions revealed how clueless the Israelite was concerning what pleased God. For God had, through the Mosaic Law, condemned human sacrifice (Lev. 18:21). Then Micah answered the questions:

> He has shown [told] you, O man, what is good; and what does the LORD require of you but to do justly, to love mercy, and to walk humbly with your God? (6:8).

The Israelite should have known what God demanded of him, for it was revealed in the Mosaic Law (Dt. 6:5; 10:12). God demanded obedience rather than sacrifice (1 Sam. 15:22; Hos.

6:6). He wanted His people to walk in justice and trust Him (1 Sam. 12:14; Hos. 12:6). Even today, the Lord is more concerned with an individual's character and conduct than with sacrifice.

Once again Micah summarized what God demanded of His people. His statement is a model of the Israelites' duty toward man and God. First, "to do justly" means to maintain honest and just relationships with one another as revealed in the Mosaic Law (Ex. 20—23; Mic. 2:1–2, 8–9; 3:1–2, 9–11). Second, "to love mercy" (Hebrew, *hesed*) expresses an attitude of loyal, covenant obedience. In divine love, God made a voluntary covenant with Israel in which He promised to be obedient to the provisions made in covenant partnership with the nation. Likewise, the Israelites were voluntarily to manifest the same attitude of loyal love and obedience to God and their fellow man. Third, "to walk humbly with your God" means they were to live circumspectly and wisely in following God's will. Micah warned the Israelites not to be careless by doing things their own way, but to do all things carefully, according to God's will. If they lived according to God's Word, they also would treat their fellow man with justice and love.

God's requirements for Israel were not negative, but positive. If followed, the Israelites would have enjoyed full lives that pleased God. God required much more from them than bringing animal sacrifices in worship. The Lord required total commitment from the heart, as revealed in His Word.

Prosperity Repudiated

After presenting Judah with God's standards, Micah exposed Jerusalem's corruption. The prophet denounced Judah's disloyalty and dishonesty: "The LORD's voice cries to the city [Jerusalem]—wisdom shall see Your name: 'Hear the rod! Who has appointed it?'" (6:9). Micah advised people to listen closely and heed what God had to say. For God had appointed a "rod" (a nation used as an instrument of His wrath) to bring judgment on Judah.

Judgment will come on the nation for three reasons. First, merchants had dishonestly and deceitfully acquired and accumulated wealth: "The treasures of wickedness [are] in the house of the wicked" (v. 10). Second, merchants had used irregular weights in doing business: "the short measure that is an abomination . . . the wicked scales, . . . the bag of deceitful weights" (vv. 10–11). Third, the inhabitants were wicked: "For her rich men are full of violence [lawlessness], her inhabitants have spoken lies, and their tongue is deceitful in their mouth" (v. 12). Injustice, insult, and a lack of integrity permeated Judean society. The wealthy set society's pattern in deceiving and defrauding the people.

Punishment Rendered

Judah's sins brought God's judgment. And the people had already starting feeling the punishments Micah was about to mention. First, sickness came on them as a result of sin: "I will also make you sick [literally, "have made"] . . . by making you desolate because of your sins" (v. 13). In Deuteronomy 28, Moses listed all the afflictions and destruction Israel would experience if it turned from serving God.

Second, the Israelites will go hungry: "You shall eat, but not be satisfied; hunger shall be in your midst" (Mic. 6:14; cf. Lev. 26:26).

Third, enemies will rifle their storehouses of food: "You may carry some away, but shall not save them" (Mic. 6:14; cf. Lev. 26:16–17; Dt. 28:33).

Fourth, they will sow crops but will not reap a harvest because they will be taken captive and not allowed to eat the fruit of their labor: "You shall sow, but not reap; . . . tread the olives, but not anoint yourselves with oil; and make sweet wine, but not drink wine" (Mic. 6:15; cf. Dt. 28:39–40).

Fifth, they are repudiated for following the sinful practices of Omri and Ahab, the two most evil kings in Israel:

> For the statutes of Omri are kept; all the works of Ahab's house are done; and you walk in their counsels, that I may make you a desolation, and your inhabitants a hissing. Therefore you shall bear the reproach of My people (Mic. 6:16).

Under these two kings, Baal worship flooded the land of Israel (1 Ki. 16:21—22:40). Even Judah followed Ahab's wicked counsel. As a result, Judah will be made desolate, and its people will be hissed at; that is, they will be scorned and ridiculed by the world (cf. Lam. 2:15–16). They will suffer reproach, or be disgraced and despised, during their captivity.

Like Judah, we each need to ask ourselves, "What does the Lord require of me?" The answer is the same. We who have trusted the Lord for our salvation need to do justly, love mercy, and walk humbly with our God. Is this the testimony of your life before God and your fellow man?

CHAPTER 30

WHO IS A GOD LIKE THE LORD!

Micah's grief over the deterioration of Judean society is poignantly expressed in this final chapter. The prophet lamented Judah's sinful condition, knowing that the nation could not go unpunished. In the midst of sorrow, Micah believed God would raise Israel from destruction.

His final message condemns the wicked and comforts the righteous. He assured the people that the day of judgment will come, but a brighter day will come as well—a day when God will fully deliver a repentant Israel and fulfill both the physical and spiritual deliverance promised in the Abrahamic Covenant.

Micah's Confession

Micah used a metaphor to lament the moral breakdown in Judean society. Like a farmer searching in vain for "summer fruits" and "like those who glean vintage grapes," Micah sought in vain for a godly man within Judah (7:1). As one who "desired the first-ripe fruit" of the harvest, his soul craved to find an honest man of integrity. But again, there was none:

The faithful [godly] man has perished from the earth, and there is no one upright among men. They all lie in wait for blood; every man hunts his brother with a net (v. 2).

Instead of treating one another with respect and civility, men lay in wait to assault or murder their neighbors, as those who would snare a bird or wild beast. In verse 3, Micah lamented the breakdown of Judah's leadership:

That they may successfully do evil with both hands—the prince asks for [demands] gifts, the judge seeks a bribe, and the great [powerful] man utters [dictates] his evil desire; so they scheme together.

These leaders used their positions and power to acquire whatever they desired. Rulers worked within the judicial system to acquire wealth from their countrymen through strong-arm tactics or by skillfully circumventing justice for financial gain—something the law forbade (Ex. 23:8; cf. Dt. 10:17). The "best" of these leaders were like "brier[s]"; and the "most upright," pricklier "than a thorn hedge" (Mic. 7:4). People who came in contact with them were torn and wounded.

The "watchmen" (prophets) foretold of judgment: "Your punishment comes; now shall be their perplexity." The word *now* emphasizes that God's judgment is soon to come; and when it does, Judah's evil leaders will be thrown into "perplexity" (v. 4). Their confidence will be destroyed, and they will become confused and confounded. This judgment fell on Jerusalem during the Babylonian invasion of 586 B.C. It also prophetically foreshadows Jerusalem's fall in the future Great Tribulation (Zech. 14:1–4).

Micah further lamented the breakdown in relationships and family. The common man in the street lacked honesty and integrity in his dealings. The land was satiated with deception, dishonesty, disloyalty, and distortion. No one could be trusted—not a friend, guide, or relative (Mic. 7:5–6). Treachery was so widespread that people had to guard their words, even to their spouses, or their spouses might turn against them.

Micah's Confidence

In light of this societal deterioration, Micah prayerfully interceded on behalf of his nation. In his prayer, he expressed confidence and hope that the Lord would deliver a righteous Jewish remnant from the midst of injustice and oppression: "I will look to the LORD; I will wait for the God of my salvation; my God will hear me" (v. 7).

The prophet focused intently on the Lord as though fixated on a watchtower, looking expectantly for God to hear his prayer and eventually bring deliverance and spiritual salvation. He anticipated a future day when God will deliver all Israel from its sin, sorrow, and subjugation. This complete fulfillment will take place after the Great Tribulation, at the Messiah's Second Coming.

Micah went on to warn Judah's enemies not to "rejoice," or gloat, over Judah's judgment and fall (v. 8). Rejoicing was premature. Identifying with Judah, Micah said,

> When I fall [face subjugation and captivity], I will arise; when I sit in darkness [spiritual darkness and affliction], the LORD will be a light to me [spiritual light to sustain and deliver a godly remnant in Israel] (v. 8).

Identifying with the sin of his people, Micah confessed, "I will bear the indignation of the LORD, because I have sinned against Him" (v. 9). It is God's indignation and wrath poured out on Judah that will eventually bring the nation back to the Lord. Micah was confident that Jehovah would "plead" the people's cause—that He would take their part, as in a court of law, and "execute justice" for them (v. 9). The prophet expected God to bring to light all the injustices perpetrated against the Jewish people throughout history. Then Judah will witness God's righteousness in repaying the nations for their anti-Semitic acts when He rights the wrongs the Jewish people have suffered throughout the centuries.

Judah's "enemy" had asked, "Where is the LORD your God?" (v. 10). These nations blasphemed God, implying that Jehovah had abandoned Judah and was unable to deliver it. But the nations that taunted Judah and Jehovah will be put to shame and "trampled down like the mud in the streets" (v. 10). Israel's enemies will be totally destroyed by the Messiah at His Second Coming (Ps. 2:1–3; Rev. 19:11—20:3).

The prophet announced that Judah and Jerusalem will be restored: "In the day when your [Jerusalem's] walls are to be built, in that day the decree shall go far and wide" (Mic. 7:11). The word *decree* is better translated by the Hebrew phrase *on that day will your boundaries be extended*. This prophecy was partially fulfilled after the Babylonian Captivity, when Jerusalem's walls were rebuilt. Its ultimate fulfillment will be during the Millennial Kingdom, when Jerusalem will be rebuilt, be expanded, and become the capital of the world.

Micah continued:

In that day they shall come to you [Jerusalem] from Assyria and the fortified cities [city of Egypt], from the fortress [also Egypt] to the River [Euphrates], from sea to sea, and mountain to mountain (v. 12; cf. Isa. 19:23–25).

This verse refers to nations coming from around the world to worship in Jerusalem during the Millennial Kingdom (cf. Mic. 4:2). Until then, both Israel and the world "shall be desolate" because God's wrath will be poured out on the earth during the Great Tribulation (7:13).

Micah's Call

Micah called on Jehovah to care once again for His people like a shepherd: "Shepherd Your people with Your staff, the flock of Your heritage . . . as in the days of old" (v. 14). The "flock of Your heritage" refers to Israel's covenant relationship with God as His special possession. Israel will be restored and ruled by the Messiah, who will be its Shepherd during the Millennium.

Then Judah will no longer be scattered throughout the nations but will dwell in its own land, as verse 14 expresses by citing the areas of Carmel, Bashan, and Gilead. In that day, Israel will be separated from the nations, live in safety, and enjoy the land promised it in the Abrahamic Covenant. Verse 15 reveals that the Lord will perform many miracles in reestablishing Israel in its land, as He did when He delivered the nation from Egyptian captivity.

As a result of these future miracles, the Gentile nations "shall see and be ashamed of all their [Israel's] might" (v. 16). The nations will become awestruck, ashamed, and alarmed at Israel's strength when God delivers it. They also will become powerless, humiliated, degraded, and disgraced. So they will "put their hand over their mouth; their ears shall be deaf" (v. 16). Thus Israel's enemies will become speechless, no longer mocking Israel and its God or closing their ears because they would not hear of the nation's victory.

In pictorial words, Micah said, "They shall lick the dust like a serpent; they shall crawl from their holes like snakes of the earth. They shall be afraid of the LORD our God, and shall fear because of You" (v. 17). In terror the nations will acknowledge and revere the Lord and prostrate themselves fearfully before Him in repentance because of His bond with Israel.

Micah's Celebration

Micah was overcome with the Lord's goodness and mercy. In the closing verses, the prophet celebrated the greatness of Jehovah. He praised the Lord by using a play on words relating to his own name: "Who is a God like You?" (v. 18). Micah's name means "Who is like the Lord?" Moses uttered the same words after God delivered Israel through the Red Sea (Ex. 15:11). Obviously, there is no other God but Jehovah; and nothing mankind worships compares to Him in the way He pardons sin and brings forgiveness and deliverance to Israel.

In the closing verses of his book, Micah's heart expressed deep gratitude to God as he gloried in the Lord's future deliverance of Israel. The prophet mentioned seven truths about God's love toward His Chosen People Israel:

1. The Lord pardons "iniquity and pass[es] over the transgression [rebellious acts] of the remnant of His heritage" (Mic. 7:18). The reference is to a remnant of Jewish people who will be protected through the Great Tribulation and saved to enter the Millennial Kingdom (Zech. 12:10; 13:9; Rom. 11:26).

2. The Lord "does not retain His anger forever" (Mic. 7:18). He is ready to show grace to the repentant.

3. The Lord "delights in mercy [loving-kindness]" (v. 18). He is ready to show compassion and forgiveness.

4. The Lord "will again have compassion on us" (v. 19). He has tender, heartfelt concern for Israel and is always ready to dispense His mercy and compassion on the nation.

5. The Lord "will subdue [tread underfoot] our iniquities" (v. 19), rendering sin powerless and inoperative, as one would an enemy.

6. The Lord will "cast all our sins into the depths of the sea" (v. 19), indicating a final end to an individual's sin, whereupon God forgives it and forgets it. Interestingly, Jewish people quote verses 18–19 on Rosh Hashanah (Jewish New

Year) when they recite this prayer of repentance in a service called *Tashlick.*

7. The Lord will "give truth [be faithful] to Jacob and mercy [loving-kindness] to Abraham, which You have sworn to our fathers from the days of old" (v. 20). Micah closed with these words that confirm the Lord will keep His promises to Israel, which He made to its forefathers in the unconditional Abrahamic Covenant.

These promises to Abraham are immutable because they were confirmed by God's sworn oath (Heb. 6:13–18). And they stand in perpetuity to the Jewish people as a source of comfort and hope to Israel today. After reading what God has done for Israel, we, too, can say, "Who is a God like the Lord!"

ENDNOTES

HOSEA

CHAPTER 1—A NATION IN DECLINE

[1] Frederick A. Tatford, "Prophet of a Broken Home," *The Minor Prophets* (Minneapolis, MN: Klock and Klock, 1982), 1:12.

[2] Gary G. Cohen and H. Ronald Vandermey, *Hosea and Amos* (Chicago: Moody Press, 1981), 12.

[3] Robert B. Chisholm Jr., "Hosea," *The Bible Knowledge Commentary: Old Testament*, ed. John F. Walvoord and Roy B. Zuck (Wheaton, Il: Victor Books, 1985), 1,379.

[4] Manfred T. Brauch, F. F. Bruce, Peter H. Davids, Walter C. Kaiser Jr., eds., *Hard Sayings of the Old Testament* (Downers Grove, Il: InterVarsity Press, 1992), 323.

AMOS

CHAPTER 16—GOD'S JUDGMENT: INEVITABLE, IRREVOCABLE

[1] Josephus, *Antiquities of the Jews*, 9.10.4.

CHAPTER 18—PREPARE TO MEET YOUR GOD

[1] Donald R. Sunukjian, "Amos," *The Bible Knowledge Commentary: Old Testament*, ed. John F. Walvoord and Roy B. Zuck (Wheaton, IL: Victor Books, 1985), 1,435.

[2] Gary G. Cohen and H. Ronald Vandermey, *Hosea and Amos* (Chicago: Moody Press, 1981), 123.

[3] W. J. Deane, "Amos," *Amos to Malachi*, vol. 14, *The Pulpit Commentary* (Grand Rapids: Eerdmans, 1950), 63.

[4] John E. Hartley, *Theological Wordbook of the Old Testament*, ed. R. Laird Harris, Gleason L. Archer Jr., and Bruce K. Waltke (Chicago: Moody Press, 1980), 2:750–751.

CHAPTER 19—SEEK GOD AND LIVE

[1] Merrill F. Unger, *Isaiah-Malachi*, vol. 2, *Unger's Commentary on the Old Testament* (Chicago: Moody Press, 1981), 1,796.

[2] Ibid.

[3] Donald R. Sunukjian, "Amos," *The Bible Knowledge Commentary: Old Testament*, ed. John F. Walvoord and Roy B. Zuck (Wheaton, IL: Victor Books, 1985), 1,442.

CHAPTER 20—A WORD TO THE WEALTHY
[1] Donald R. Sunukjian, "Amos," *The Bible Knowledge Commentary: Old Testament*, ed. John F. Walvoord and Roy B. Zuck (Wheaton, IL: Victor Books, 1985), 1,443.

CHAPTER 21—THE FATAL VISION
[1] Ralph Blodgett, "Can Psychics and Astrologers Predict the Future?" *Vibrant Life* (July/August 1986), 14.
[2] Donald R. Sunukjian, "Amos," *The Bible Knowledge Commentary: Old Testament*, ed. John F. Walvoord and Roy B. Zuck (Wheaton, IL: Victor Books, 1985), 1,446.
[3] Ibid., 1,446.
[4] Ibid., 1,447.

CHAPTER 22—A DYING DYNASTY
[1] Theo Laetsch, "Amos," *The Minor Prophets* (St. Louis, MO: Concordia Publishing, 1956), 181.
[2] Homer Hailey, "Amos," *A Commentary on the Minor Prophets* (Grand Rapids: Baker Book House, 1972), 121.
[3] E. B. Pusey, "Amos," *The Minor Prophets* (Grand Rapids: Baker Book House, 1950), 1:328.
[4] Gary G. Cohen and H. Ronald Vandermey, *Hosea and Amos* (Chicago: Moody Press, 1981), 159.
[5] "About Our Shield and Logo," Harvard Graduate School of Arts and Sciences Christian Community <hcs.harvard.edu/~gsascf/shield.html>.

CHAPTER 23—A NATION OF DYNASTY
[1] Herbert Lockyer, *The Romantic History of Israel* (Winona Lake, IN: American Association for Jewish Evangelism), 4–7, 12.
[2] Theo Laetsch, "Amos," *The Minor Prophets* (St. Louis, MO: Concordia Publishing, 1956), 183.
[3] C. I. Scofield, *The New Scofield Reference Bible* (New York: Oxford University Press, 1967), 937 n. Amos 9:1.
[4] Merrill F. Unger, "Isaiah-Malachi," *Unger's Commentary on the Old Testament* (Chicago: Moody Press, 1981), 1:1,1807.

RECOMMENDED READING

Boice, James Montgomery. *The Minor Prophets*. Grand Rapids: Kregel Publications, 1983.

Bullock, C Hassell. *An Introduction to the Old Testament Prophetic Books*. Chicago: Moody Press, 1986.

Cohen, Gary G., and Ronald H. Vandermey. *Hosea and Amos*. Chicago: Moody Press, 1981.

Feinberg, Charles L. *The Minor Prophets*. Chicago: Moody Press, 1976.

Finley, Thomas J. *Everyman's Bible Commentary: Joel, Obadiah, and Micah*. *Chicago:* Moody Press, 1996.

Freeman, Hobart E. *An Introduction to the Old Testament Prophets*. Chicago: Moody Press. 1968.

Ironside, H. A. *Notes on the Minor Prophets*. Neptune, NJ: Loizeaux Brothers, 1909.

Kaiser, Walter C., et al. *Hard Sayings of the Bible*. Downer's Grove, Ill: InterVarsity Press, 1992.

Kaiser, Walter C. *The Preacher's Commentary Series*. Vol. 23, *Micah–Malachi*. Nashville: Thomas Nelson Publishers, 1992.

Keil, C. F. *Biblical Commentary on the Old Testament: Minor Prophets*. Grand Rapids: Eerdmans, 1949.

Laetsch, Theo. *Bible Commentary: The Minor Prophets*. St. Louis: Concordia Publishing House, 1956.

Ogilvie, Lloyd J. *The Preacher's Commentary Series*. Vol. 22, *Hosea/Joel/Amos/Obadiah/Jonah*. Nashville: Thomas Nelson Publishers, 1990.

Phillips, John. *Exploring the Minor Prophets: The Book of the Twelve*. Neptune, NJ: Loizeaux Brothers, 1998.

Pusey, E. B. *The Minor Prophets: A Commentary*. Grand Rapids: Baker Book House, 1950.

Tatford, Frederick A. *The Minor Prophets*. Reprint, Minneapolis: Klock and Klock, 1982.

Unger, Merrill F. *Unger's Commentary on the Old Testament*. Vol. 2. Chicago: Moody Press, 1981.

Walvoord, John F., and Roy B. Zuck. *The Bible Knowledge Commentary*. Vol. 1. Wheaton: Victor Books, 1985.

Walvoord, John F. *The Prophecy Knowledge Handbook*. Wheaton: Victor Books, 1990.

Daniel and Minor Prophets With Wycliffe Bible Commentary. New York: The Iversen-Norman Associates, 1975.

OTHER BOOKS BY DAVID M. LEVY

GUARDING THE GOSPEL OF GRACE
We often lack peace, joy, or victory in our walk with Christ because we're not clear how God's grace works in our lives. The books of Galatians and Jude are brought together in this marvelous work that explains grace and what can happen if you stray from it. Don't miss out on the difference that God's grace can make in your life. It's nothing less than amazing!

ISBN-10: 0-915540-26-6, ISBN-13: 978-0-915540-26-6, #B67

JOEL: THE DAY OF THE LORD
What lies in store for the nations of the world? Learn what God has planned concerning the destinies of nations as they relate to Israel in the Day of the Lord. Illustrated chapter outlines and graphics give added insight into the timely and dynamic book of Joel, which surely is one of the most neglected and misinterpreted in the Bible.

ISBN-10: 0-915540-37-1, ISBN-13: 978-0-915540-37-2, #B32

MALACHI: MESSENGER OF REBUKE AND RENEWAL
Whatever the need—social, political, or religious—you'll find the answer in this verse-by-verse, nontechnical exposition that deals with contemporary issues while providing a comprehensive chronology of Israel's prophetic history.

ISBN-10: 0-915540-20-7, ISBN-13: 978-0-915540-20-4, #B45

REVELATION: HEARING THE LAST WORD
Why is there so much uncertainty and disagreement about the last days? What can we know about the Antichrist? What is the order of the end-times events? What about Israel? What will life be like in the Millennial Kingdom? This valuable resource will help you know what to expect as Earth's final hour approaches.

ISBN-10: 0-915540-60-6, ISBN-13: 978-0-915540-60-0, #B75

THE TABERNACLE: SHADOWS OF THE MESSIAH

Explore Israel's wilderness Tabernacle, the service of the priesthood, and the significance of the sacrifices. Excellent illustrations will open new vistas of biblical truth as ceremonies, sacrifices, and priestly service reveal the perfections of the Messiah.

ISBN-10: 0-915540-17-7, ISBN-13: 978-0-915540-17-4, #B51

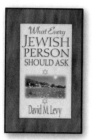

WHAT EVERY JEWISH PERSON SHOULD ASK

Can I know God? Why do I feel alienated from God? What can good works do for me? Is there really a Messiah? What decisions must I make about my spiritual life? If you need answers to life's most important questions, this excellent book is a must-read.

ISBN-10: 0-915540-81-9, ISBN-13: 978-0-915540-81-5, # B81

WHEN PROPHETS SPEAK OF JUDGMENT: HABAKKUK, ZEPHANIAH, HAGGAI

Is our nation on the brink of judgment? In this fascinating overview of Habakkuk, Zephaniah, and Haggai, you'll discover that the very conditions that led to Judah's downfall are all present in America today. This volume explores these conditions and challenges us to "redeem the time" as we move ever closer to the last days.

ISBN-10: 0-915540-35-5, ISBN-13: 978-0-915540-35-8, #B70